Devotions

FOR DATING COUPLES

OTHER BOOKS BY
BEN YOUNG AND DR. SAMUEL ADAMS

The Ten Commandments of Dating
The One

Devotions

FOR DATING COUPLES

Building a Foundation of Spiritual Intimacy

BEN YOUNG & DR. SAMUEL ADAMS

THOMAS NELSON PUBLISHERS®
Nashville

A Division of Thomas Nelson, Inc.
www.ThomasNelson.com

Published in Nashville, Tennessee, by Thomas Nelson, Inc.

Unless otherwise noted, Scripture quotations are from the HOLY BIBLE: NEW INTERNATIONAL VERSION®. Copyright © 1973, 1978, 1984 by International Bible Society. Used by permission of Zondervan Publishing House. All rights reserved.

Scripture quotations noted KJV are from the KING JAMES VERSION.

Scripture quotations noted *The Message* are from *The Message: The New Testament in Contemporary English.* Copyright © 1993 by Eugene H. Peterson.

Scripture quotations noted PHILLIPS are from J. B. Phillips: THE NEW TESTAMENT IN ENGLISH, Revised Edition. Copyright © J. B. Phillips 1958, 1960, 1972. Used by permission of Macmillan Publishing Co., Inc.

Scripture quotations noted NKJV are from THE NEW KING JAMES VERSION. Copyright © 1979, 1980, 1982, Thomas Nelson Publishers.

Scripture quotations noted NLT are from the *Holy Bible,* New Living Translation, copyright © 1996. Used by permission of Tyndale House Publishers, Inc., Wheaton, Illinois 60189. All rights reserved.

Scripture quotations noted NASB are from the NEW AMERICAN STANDARD BIBLE®, © Copyright The Lockman Foundation 1960, 1962, 1963, 1968, 1971, 1972, 1973, 1975, 1977. Used by permission.

Library of Congress Cataloging-in-Publication Data

Young, Ben.
    Devotions for dating couples : building a foundation of spiritual intimacy / Ben Young & Sam Adams
        p. cm.
    ISBN 0-7852-6749-2 (pbk.)
    1. Single people—Religious life. 2. Dating (Social Customs)—Religious aspects—Christianity. I. Adams, Sam. II. Title.

BV4596.S5 Y68 2002
248.8'4—dc21   2001054382

Printed in the United States of America

02 03 04 05 PHX 5 4 3 2 1

To our parents, Ed and Jo Beth Young
and Alex and Paula Adams—thank you
for leading us to salvation and showing
us the value of a daily walk with God.

CONTENTS

Devotions

FOR DATING COUPLES

*H*ave you ever stopped to consider how much time, energy, and emotion you spend on your outer self, the externals of life? Think about it. The overwhelming majority of your life is spent on the externals—making money, eating, exercising, entertaining, shopping, sleeping, and so on. Such focus and attention are legitimate and even necessary for basic living. However, in contrast, consider how much attention you give to your inner life. How much time do you actually spend nurturing your soul? Is your relationship with God a priority? If it is, then this devotional will guide you toward a more active, ongoing relationship with your Creator, God.

Devotions for Dating Couples is designed to encourage you to take a look inside and focus more deliberately on your inner life. First and foremost, it is a resource to help you enhance and nourish your spiritual life and your personal relationship with God. There is no greater endeavor than the process of developing a deeper connection with God. This guide will lead you on your spiritual journey.

In addition, this devotional is a resource to help serious dating couples (or engaged couples) begin to build a foundation of spiritual intimacy in order to promote the kind of marriage that will last a lifetime. We are convinced that the essence of a true soul mate relationship is that of deep spiritual connection. Unfortunately far too many people are merely concerned with finding a companion or a playmate rather than a soul mate. A true soul mate relationship can be attained only when there are a solid level of spiritual compatibility and a mutual agreement that the marriage centers on a relationship with God. Once you find a partner who has the potential for a true soul mate relationship, then you can start to lay a foundation of spiritual intimacy upon which to build in years to come.

This resource is for couples who are in a long-term dating relationship with a view toward marriage. It is not necessarily intended for couples who are casually dating or in the early stages of a relationship. In fact, it's possible to develop spiritual intimacy too soon before a relationship has the opportunity to grow more naturally. Therefore, we advise you to be cautious and mindful of this danger. In our book *The Ten Commandments of Dating*, we warn couples to take their relationship slowly and allow for a natural bonding to take place over time. We offer seven slow-motion dating strategies, one of which is the need to avoid praying together until the relationship has a chance to grow and develop in other areas. In the spirit of this principle, we suggest that spiritual intimacy should be reserved for committed couples in the later stages of the relationship, committed couples who have their eyes on marriage.

A USER-FRIENDLY GUIDE

We hope to make this devotional a user-friendly guide that enables you to explore core issues of spirituality. We're not interested in confusing you with profound theological conundrums, nor are we concerned with trivial or nonessential religious legalism—they just complicate true spirituality. Our focus is on the basic, foundational aspects of spirituality: the Christian virtues and practices of love, grace, prayer, Bible study, simplicity, forgiveness, community, purity, and living in the power of the Holy Spirit.

A significant part of the process of developing a rich, rewarding spiritual life is just a matter of showing up and paying attention. It's not so much about "doing" more for God; it's about "being" in His presence. When we make ourselves available to God, to listen to the whisper of His Spirit, or when we put ourselves in positions of solitude and simply allow ourselves to be still and know, we make room for God to be a part of our lives. Only when we take out the distractions of our chaotic lives do we allow God to participate in transforming our lives and relationships into all He intended them to be.

HOW TO USE THIS DEVOTIONAL

This devotional is designed to be used daily for nine weeks. Each week is devoted to one primary discipline or area. The first five days of the week (Monday through Friday) will challenge you on your individual walk with God and should be done alone. At the end of each daily devotional there is a place for further meditation on designated portions of Scriptures. The Christian version of meditation is about reflection and focus on a particular topic. Far from the Eastern version of meditation, which encourages you to empty your mind, this form of meditation encourages you to fill your mind with the things of God and then take the time to reflect or chew on them. Doing this allows you to redirect your attention toward God's principles and truths.

Of course, we want you to be prayerful as you study and read Scripture during these nine weeks. We have provided a section at the end of each week devoted to prayer. We have found that having some form of structure during a prayer time is helpful. Feel free to use the suggested outline (P.R.A.Y.). In addition, please use the space provided to write down or journal your thoughts and prayers to God.

Saturday is reserved for you and your partner to answer questions and share insights from the previous week of study together. We hope to stimulate meaningful discussion between yourselves about the most important aspects of the Christian faith. Keep in mind that the ultimate goal of this devotional is to enhance your relationship with God, both as individuals and as a couple. Our prayer is that God will use this study to stimulate growth, to bless you with fresh insights, and to encourage a deeper walk with Him.

Sunday provides the opportunity for you and your partner to attend church together. We are convinced that one of the greatest ways to enhance spiritual compatibility is to praise and worship God together with a group of believers. Furthermore, church attendance can be a catalyst for sharing with each other the things that God may be teaching you. We have provided a place for you to take notes on the sermon/message for that day as well as any relevant insights to discuss at a later point.

We are certain that God relentlessly pursues a closer relationship with you, and to that end, He is not hard to find.

Eugene Peterson said it best in *The Message:* "Starting from scratch, [God] made the entire human race and made the earth hospitable, with plenty of time and space for living so we could seek after God, and not just grope around in the dark but actually find him. He doesn't play hide-and-seek with us. He's not remote; he's near." You see, God is always waiting for you with open arms, and He longs for a deeper connection. So come along and let us encourage you on the spiritual path toward a deeper relationship with eternal God.

Love

They do not love that do not show their love.

—WILLIAM SHAKESPEARE

We must grow in love and in order to do this we
must go on loving and loving and giving and
giving until it hurts—the way Jesus did.
Do ordinary things with extraordinary love.

—MOTHER TERESA

Love has nothing to do with what you are expected to get.
It's what you are expected to give.

—ANONYMOUS

True Love

This is love: not that we loved God, but that he loved us and sent his Son as an atoning sacrifice for our sins . . . And so we know and rely on the love God has for us. God is love. Whoever lives in love lives in God, and God in him.

—1 JOHN 4:10, 16

Do you remember when you fell in love? That first glance? The first time you held hands? The thought, *Could this be the one?* Few things on this earth can compare with that magical experience (most of which are illegal). Let's face it. The feeling of romantic love is flat-out intoxicating. I remember that initial connection with my wife, Julie, when I thought, *Nothing could be better than this!*

You know what? I was dead wrong. Oh, sure, that passionate love was great (and it still is). Passion and romance are certainly legitimate forms of love and important in the process of bringing men and women together. But passionate love is just a taste of something better. It points us to a higher love, a true love. Believe it or not, there is a love that runs deeper, stronger, and truer than any form of earthly romance—God's love.

God is not only the Author and Designer of love; He is the

very essence of this thing we call love. He is the pure Embodiment of genuine love. Therefore, it stands to reason that our need to love and to be loved must first begin with Him. Now this may sound strange at first (especially for men), but do you realize that God essentially wants to engage each of us in a love affair? In fact, did you know that your deepest longing is to be caught up in a love relationship with God? As Brent Curtis and John Eldredge suggested in their book, *The Sacred Romance,* "This longing is the most powerful part of our personality. It fuels our search for meaning, for wholeness, for a sense of being truly alive. However we describe this deep desire, it is the most important thing about us, our heart of hearts, the passion of our lives." No human relationship can fill the void deep within. Certainly no material possession can satisfy the longing. It is only through an abiding love relationship with God that we experience a true sense of completion and wholeness.

God's love to you in Christ Jesus is *unconditional*. It's refreshing to know that His love comes with no strings attached, no hidden agenda or ulterior motives. God's love is *stable* and enduring, unlike forms of earthly love, which are temporary and fleeting at best. God's love is *perfect*. It is sufficient to meet all your needs for acceptance, worth, or value. Best of all, God's love is *permanent*. Paul wrote in Romans 8:38–39: "For I am convinced that neither death nor life, neither angels nor demons, neither the present nor the future, nor any powers, neither height nor depth, nor anything else in all creation, will be able to separate us from the love of God that is in Christ Jesus our Lord."

What do you know about God's love? Can you honestly say that you have personally experienced true love from above? If you already have this love relationship with God, then take time now to thank Him for the love that only He can provide and reflect upon the permanence of this true love. If you do not know this love, make it your desire today to establish a love relationship with God through Jesus Christ and begin the greatest romance of your life.

FURTHER SCRIPTURAL MEDITATION

- John 15:9–10 *As the father has loved me, so have I loved you*
- 1 John 3:1, 16
- 1 John 4:7–21 *love lives in God & God*

John 15:17

"This is my command love each other"

"Whoever lives in ~~believes lives lives~~ in him"

Summarize, in your own words, the essence of this day's devotional on love. Write down any thoughts, feelings, or insights in the space below.

Dear God, thank You that Your love for me is permanent and unconditional. Teach me to fully experience this True Love and may I seek to pass it on to those around me. Amen.

First Love ♡

"Love the Lord your God with all your heart and with all your soul and with all your mind and with all your strength." The second is this: "Love your neighbor as yourself." There is no commandment greater than these.

—MARK 12:30–31

We were sitting there minding our own business on the back row when all of a sudden, a newly engaged couple came in and sat down right in front of us, giggling and whispering sweet nothings to each other. Fused together like Siamese twins, the oblivious couple couldn't seem to keep their hands off each other. To make matters worse, we weren't in a movie theater or concert hall. We had to witness this inappropriate exhibition of PDA (public display of affection) in church!

During this wonderful worship service, while the rest of the congregation was praising God through music and song, I was struck by the irony of what was taking place right in front of me. The young man and young woman were so engrossed with themselves that they missed out on the most meaningful and significant love experience in life—praising and worshiping their God. In a sense, they were caught up in their own private "worship" service between themselves. They were worshiping each other rather than the Creator. I was just about to tell them to cool it when they got up and left the service. Whew! Let's face it. There is a time and a place for everything, but that certainly wasn't it.

Indeed, love starts with God. He is the Initiator, and the only way we can truly love is to receive His love first (we love because He first loved us). Once we accept His gift of love, we must reciprocate that love to God—and then to others as a natural overflow. He deserves our highest devotion and our deepest adoration. We are all created with a built-in desire to worship something or someone.

The question is, How do you channel your appetite for worship? At any given moment you are devoted to something or someone, whether or not you are aware of it. Your thoughts, words, and actions will reveal what is truly in your heart of hearts. God wants you to be fully devoted to Him; to love Him first and to do so with your whole life.

Consider what God says in Deuteronomy 5:7 (KJV): "Thou shalt have none other gods before me." That's about as definitive as you can get! When asked about the greatest commandment, Jesus declared that our affections belong to God first and foremost. So, whom do you worship? Perhaps the strongest temptation that you face as a dating partner or an engaged couple is the tendency to worship your partner or even love itself. Don't get me wrong. I remember my own days of worshiping my partner on the "back row." It's great to enjoy each other and the relationships with which God has blessed you, but you must not elevate anyone or anything above God Himself. Just as all great works of art point us to the artist, so, too, all great love relationships should point us to a deeper love for God.

When you establish that God is your first priority, your primary focus, indeed your first love, then you are in the very best position to love someone else. Do you want to be a great lover? Do you want to enhance your capacity to love here on earth? Then make sure your first love is God.

FURTHER SCRIPTURAL MEDITATION
- Luke 7:36–50
- Romans 8:31–39
- Ephesians 1:3–8

Summarize, in your own words, the essence of this day's devotional on love. Write down any thoughts, feelings, or insights in the space below.

Dear Lord, enable me to keep my thoughts and focus on You first and foremost. God, please use me as an instrument of Your love. Amen.

Keeping Love Alive

As the deer pants for streams of water,
so my soul pants for you, O God.
My soul thirsts for God, for the living God.
When can I go and meet with God?

—PSALM 42:1–2

I'm continually astonished at the number of people who come into the office for relationship advice and share this simple desire: "I want a low-maintenance relationship. I don't want to have to work too hard!" Everyone wants intimate friendships, but not everyone is willing to cultivate and maintain these types of relationships. Let me set the record straight: close relationships don't just "happen," and they are certainly not self-sustaining. By its very nature any healthy, vibrant, intimate friendship requires work, regular interaction, and quality time together. This applies across the board, including romantic relationships, close friendships, and even relationships with family members.

My friendships are valuable to me, and I work hard to cultivate intimacy and maintain a sense of connection with each friend. I put a lot of time, energy, and emotion into my relationships. Regularly I telephone my close friends to check in; I affirm their value and importance to me; I arrange to meet them for lunch or some sporting event; I listen to them, encourage them, and pray for them; I lean on them and constantly ask for their support. And guess what? They do the same. It's our way of keeping the friendship alive. This "friendship maintenance" is a necessity, and it's something I look forward to doing. Without this process the flame of our relationship becomes a flicker and eventually dies.

Keeping the love alive with God is much the same. It is not necessarily automatic. It requires an intentional effort and some degree of planning. We must plan for success in the relationship with God, just as we are deliberate and we faithfully set aside time with a sweetheart here on earth. Making the opportunity to get away from the hustle and bustle of life and its demands is vital to growth and spiritual strengthening.

Let me say it again. Carving out time to spend with God in quiet solitude is a nonnegotiable component of a healthy spiritual life. God is not going to show up in the flesh for dinner, a movie, and a late-night stroll in the park. Therefore, you must sustain your special relationship with God by using such practices as prayer, meditation, reflection, solitude, and Bible study. Engaging in these spiritual endeavors fans the spiritual flame and keeps the love alive.

How often do you plan to meet with God, to share intimately with Him? Is this something that you engage in just on Sunday mornings or religious holidays? I hope not. Keeping the spiritual flame ignited must be a regular, daily process. Consider King David, the gifted psalmist, who often arose early in the morning to meet with God ("In the morning, O

LORD, you hear my voice; in the morning I lay my requests before you and wait in expectation" [Psalm 5:3]).

Or think about your love relationship and the endless preoccupation with finding time to be together. What would happen to your friendship if you just blew each other off for days at a time? What if you saw each other haphazardly or randomly every two or three weeks? I'll tell you what would happen: you wouldn't make it. Your relationship would fizzle.

How would you evaluate your relationship with God? What are the obstacles that keep you from connecting regularly with Him? What are the methods (spiritual activities) that help you nurture your intimacy with God? Your time with God is essential for spiritual health. Make sure it is a priority.

FURTHER SCRIPTURAL MEDITATION

- Matthew 22:36–39
- Colossians 3:12–15
- Ephesians 5:1–2

Summarize, in your own words, the essence of this day's devotional on love. Write down any thoughts, feelings, or insights in the space below.

Father, my desire is to seek You daily. Inspire me to nurture our relationship and keep the spiritual flame alive. Amen.

Love in Action

This is love: not that we loved God, but that he loved us and sent his Son as an atoning sacrifice for our sins. Dear friends, since God so loved us, we also ought to love one another . . . God lives in us and his love is made complete in us.

—1 JOHN 4:10–12

*I*magine for a moment that you embark on a mountain-climbing expedition somewhere in the Colorado Rockies with your good friend. At some point along the way, you lose your footing and find yourself in the precarious position of dangling off the edge of an icy two-hundred-foot cliff by one finger (let's make this dramatic). You are screaming for your friend, crying out for help.

But he doesn't reach down to help you. Instead your hiking buddy begins to eloquently intellectualize and verbalize his love toward you. He even begins to experience all kinds of wonderful, blissful feelings about how much he loves you and how much he will miss you when you fall to your death on the rocks below. He tilts his head ever so slightly, bites his lip, and says, "I love you so much. I'm just overwhelmed with loving feelings toward you right now."

Would you call that love? Of course not! You would most certainly call that something other than love—maybe cruelty, apathy, or hatred. Yet so often we define love as some nebulous emotion or sentimental words when in reality, love is so much more than feelings. Love is primarily manifested through action. Love is something you do.

Poets, philosophers, and theologians have tried to unravel the mysteries of love in an attempt to arrive at a precise definition. And certainly many wise things have been said about love. But to really understand love in its purest form, we must go to the Author of love.

God is Love. And He decided to display this love through the most dramatic act in human history—the ultimate demonstration of love—Christ's death on the cross. There is no greater example of love than Christ's sacrifice on that rugged cross some two thousand years ago. It would take the coldest hearts to be unmoved by this dramatic demonstration. From this, we understand and appreciate the fundamental characteristics of real love.

First, it shows us that *love is an action*. Real love is not merely a thought, a feeling, or undemonstrated words; rather, it manifests itself through action. God *demonstrated* His love; God *sent* His Son. These are action words. True love isn't demonstrated until your hiking partner risks his life to extend a hand and pull you to safety. That's genuine love!

Second, *true love is sacrificial*. It includes some element of selfless giving, putting aside your own needs for the sake of another. When God gave up His *one and only* Son as payment for the sin of the world, He essentially gave up a part of Himself.

Third, this genuine form of *love is transforming*. True love is such that it has the potential to change others' lives for the better. Touching others with true love creates the opportunity for some kind of growth, change, or maturity. Back to our ultimate example, God loved us by giving us His Son. When you accept and embrace His gift of love, the result is transforming; you have new life, restored relationship with God, and access to the power that raised Christ from the dead. You are literally in a process of changing from the inside out.

That's what true love is all about. Ask God to help you love others with that selfless, genuine form of love. We challenge you to begin with your intimate friendships, especially your dating partner. Show the kind of love that seeks the highest good in him or her. Remember, *love* is a verb, so go out and do it!

FURTHER SCRIPTURAL MEDITATION

- John 14:21–24
- 1 John 4:7–21
- 1 John 5:2–3

Summarize, in your own words, the essence of this day's devotional on love. Write down any thoughts, feelings, or insights in the space below.

Lord, thank You for demonstrating Your love by sending me Your Son. Thank You for this example of sacrificial love. Help me to exhibit this kind of love toward my partner. Amen.

The Source of Love

If you remain in me and my words remain in you, ask whatever you wish, and it will be given you. This is to my Father's glory, that you bear much fruit, showing yourselves to be my disciples.

—JOHN 15:7–8

As a newlywed in the first few years of marriage, I (Sam) recall attending a good friend's wedding, hearing the famous love passage in 1 Corinthians 13. If I've heard it once, I've heard it a thousand times: "Love is patient, love is kind. It does not envy, it does not boast, it is not proud. It is not rude, it is not self-seeking, it is not easily angered, it keeps no record of wrongs. Love does not delight in evil but rejoices with the truth. It always protects, always trusts, always hopes, always perseveres. Love never fails" (vv. 4–8).

I sat there thinking, *Yeah, right! This is real nice and poetic, but nobody can love like that. It's just impossible to live up to those standards!* When I sat through yet another wedding ceremony and reflected on the ideals of love, I felt guilty and ashamed. Deep down I knew I wasn't capable of loving my sweet, new wife with that kind of love.

To illustrate even further, let's consider all the requirements of a sacrificial love in marriage. It's exhausting to contemplate all the things I am required to do as a Christian husband. These expectations are extraordinary and impossible to fulfill. For starters, I'm commanded to love my wife as Christ loves the church; to lay down my life for her (oh, that's an easy one!). I'm called to make sacrifices for her; to put her needs above mine. In addition, I'm supposed to accept, affirm, appreciate, challenge, comfort, encourage, forgive, inspire, lead, respect, support, and validate her. And to top it all off, she wants me to share my feelings from time to time!

It was a relief to discover, several years later, that I wasn't supposed to be able to love anyone like that. God has no expectations for me to love this way on my own. He must do these things through me. When my relationship with God is stable, these loving qualities flow through me. When I am spiritually distant and attempting to live life on my own or according to my own agenda, I fail miserably in my attempts. Therefore I must keep my focus predominantly on staying connected, tapped into the Source of love. In the gospel of John, Jesus said, "I am the vine; you are the branches. If a man remains in me and I in him, he will bear much fruit; apart from me you can do nothing" (15:5).

Christ used the vine and branch illustration to represent our need to stay connected to Him daily, hourly, even minute by minute. Christ identified Himself as the "true vine" (John 15:1), and we (as Christians) are the branches. The vine gives life and sustenance to the branch and allows it to grow and bear fruit. It's no exaggeration to say that we are often inadequate, insufficient, and utterly dependent upon Christ to live His life through us every day. Only through Christ can we bear the fruit of the Spirit.

Do you want to love as Christ loves us? Want to be able to serve, forgive, inspire your partner? Want to have joy, peace, or patience? Then make it your goal to stay connected to "the vine," that is, Christ. Experiment with this foundational principle and you, too, will reap the rewards (bear the fruit) that can be gained only by staying connected to the Power Source—the Vine.

FURTHER SCRIPTURAL MEDITATION
- 1 Corinthians 13:1–13
- Philippians 1:3–5
- Colossians 1:27–29

Summarize, in your own words, the essence of this day's devotional on love. Write down any thoughts, feelings, or insights in the space below.

Dear Father, teach me to stay connected to You moment by moment. Forgive me when I try to be self sufficient; help me to rely upon You, You alone, for my strength. Amen.

Prayer

Dear God,

Thank You for Your overwhelming love for me. Lord, You are the beginning, the very definition, and the perfect example of real love. I thank You that You first loved me and demonstrated Your love not just in words but in the sacrificial gift of Your Son, Jesus Christ.

Lord, I confess that my love and devotion are often misdirected away from You, the only deserving object of my affection, to other people, relationships, hopes, and dreams. I confess that I often pay only lip service to You, claiming to be a disciple of Christ with my words and emotions but not demonstrating my discipleship in action.

Help me to better comprehend and receive the depths of Your love for me that I might better be able to respond to You with authentic love, and that Your abundant love might overflow from my heart to those around me as well. Please teach me how to love You appropriately in my actions; to grow beyond mere religion to a deep and abiding relationship with You. You have taught me this week that I am not capable of sufficiently loving You and others without Your help. Please empower me by the Holy Spirit as I strive to stay connected to You through prayer, Your Word, and the Holy Spirit.

In Jesus' name I pray. Amen.

PRAISE (ADORATION):

REPENTANCE (CONFESSION):

APPRECIATION (THANKSGIVING):

YIELD (REQUESTS):

A Foundation of Love

*T*oday we would like to encourage you and your partner to set aside some time just for the two of you. Perhaps you can go out to lunch, drive to the park, or get away to some other setting that might be conducive to discussing the foundation of *love*. Keep in mind that the purpose is to ask questions, listen with compassion, and share with each other about your experiences regarding the issue for this past week. This is not a time to debate or argue about theological perspectives. This is a time to listen and seek to understand each other with a spirit of support and encouragement. Ultimately this venture together is intended to build a stronger foundation of spiritual intimacy.

This past week we have been exploring the topic of love, particularly God's love. You have identified the Source of love and the characteristics of true love. You have been encouraged to keep your love relationship with God a priority over everything and everyone else on this earth. And you have discovered that the only way to love your partner with a genuine, sacrificial kind of love is to stay connected to the Source—that is, Jesus Christ. The greatest lovers are those who abide (live) in Christ daily and allow themselves to be instruments of God's powerful love.

QUESTIONS FOR DISCUSSION

1. Are you ever tempted to elevate your partner or your love relationship over God Himself?

2. How can your partner challenge you in your relationship with God to keep it first and foremost?

3. What can you do to exhibit a more godly form of love toward your partner?

4. How can you inspire each other to express a genuine form of love toward others?

5. Are you more spiritually in tune or motivated as a result of your relationship together? Are you drawn closer to God? Why or why not?

6. Which devotional from the last five days on the topic of love was most inspiring or convicting for you? Do you have any other strong feelings or reactions from this week's topic?

SUNDAY

(TODAY'S DATE)

SERMON NOTES:

INSIGHTS TO SHARE:

Grace

To live by grace means to acknowledge my whole life story,
the light side and the dark.

—BRENNAN MANNING

Amazing grace, how sweet the sound
that saved a wretch like me . . .
'tis grace hath brought me safe thus far,
and grace will lead me home.

—JOHN NEWTON

We are worthy of being believed only as we are
aware of our unworthiness.

—KARL BARTH

Running the Race with Grace

Are you so foolish? After beginning with the Spirit, are you now trying to attain your goal by human effort?

—GALATIANS 3:3

One of the greatest movies ever made is *Chariots of Fire*. It is a real-life story of two British track stars and their quest for an Olympic gold medal. One of these men, Eric Liddell, is a Scottish minister who has the legs of a racehorse and the heart of a champion. His rival competitor is a talented, but embittered runner named Harold Abrahams. Liddell runs with a charismatic passion because he is racing to the glory of God. Abrahams is running to gain a sense of approval and acceptance. He is stuck on the performance treadmill of life.

The contrast throughout the film is stark—one man is running with great joy and ease because he knows the acceptance of his heavenly Father. The other man is running to prove his very existence and worth as a human being.

Often in our spiritual trek we start off enjoying the amazing grace of God on a regular basis. But somewhere along the way we get tripped up, and instead of relating to God on the basis of grace, we revert to a performance mentality. We swallow the lie that says, "You are saved by grace, but you earn God's blessings in your life on a daily basis by your works." In other words grace is for unbelievers and the law is for believers. Nothing could be farther from the truth.

Sometimes I (Ben) slip back into the performance mentality before I speak at a conference or in church. As I get up to speak, I catch myself checking my spiritual pulse: *Let's see. Did I pray today? Did I read the Bible? Did I witness to the person seated next to me on the plane?* On some occasions I'll think, *This is going to be a lousy message. There is no way God could bless this after all the things I did today and the things I didn't do as well.* On other occasions I'll reason internally, *Hmmm. It has been a great day. I read my Bible, prayed (on my knees no less), and even took out the trash. God is certainly going to smile on my message tonight!* In both situations I was relating to God on the basis of my performance instead of His grace. In scenario number one, I felt that I had forfeited God's blessing, and in scenario number two, I felt that I had merited His blessing.

God never intended for you to relate to Him on the basis of your good day–bad day performance. Your performance is never good enough to be acceptable to Him. Jerry Bridges says it so beautifully in his book *The Discipline of Grace:* "Your worst days are never so bad that you are beyond the reach of God's grace. And your best days are never so good that you are beyond the need of God's grace." Grace is not just for beginners; it is for you and for me. As the old hymn "Amazing Grace" puts it:

Through many dangers, toils, and snares,
I have already come;
'tis grace hath brought me safe thus far,
and grace will lead me home.

What about you? Are you living a life caught in the performance trap, or are you experiencing the joy of running the race with grace?

FURTHER SCRIPTURAL MEDITATION
- Galatians 2:20–21
- Philippians 1:3, 6
- 2 Peter 3:18

Summarize, in your own words, the essence of this day's devotional on grace. Write down any thoughts, feelings, or insights in the space below.

Dear God, thank You for Your amazing grace for me. Help me to live each moment of every day dependent upon Your grace. Amen.

Cheap Grace

What shall we say, then? Shall we go on sinning so that grace may increase? By no means! We died to sin; how can we live in it any longer?

—ROMANS 6:1–2

*O*nce saved, always saved" has to be one of the most abused and misused statements in Christianity. The original meaning assures you that once you have received God's grace through Jesus Christ, you can never lose your salvation. The popular meaning of this slogan is that you can pray a prayer to receive Jesus and then live any way you want and still go to heaven. In other words as long as you have "prayed the prayer," you can live like hell here on earth and still go to that deluxe apartment in the sky when you die. German martyr Dietrich Bonhoeffer called this mentality "cheap grace."

This cheap grace theology has been around the Christian faith for two thousand years. When the apostle Paul penned these words to a group of Christians in Rome in A.D. 55, he was combating this same heresy, properly dubbed *antinomianism*. Antinomians were people who were against the law. They reasoned that since you can't earn God's grace and your sins just serve as a backdrop to accentuate God's grace, then why not sin all the more so that more grace can be given? Paul was answering this charge in the sixth chapter of Romans. He said, "How in the world can we keep on sinning if through Christ, we are dead to our sins? If God has given us the very righteousness of His Son, then why would we desire to tarnish His gift?"

If someone gave you a brand-new, tailor-made, 100 percent silk white jacket, you would not want to go out and roll around in a mud puddle with it. To the contrary, you would do everything in your power to keep it as clean as possible.

This idea applies to your relationship with God as well. He has credited Christ's perfect righteousness to your account and placed His Holy Spirit in your heart. Who would intentionally take this gift for granted? Now you will still sin, and at times the desire to sin may even be much greater than your desire to obey God. However, as a believer, you will confess your sin, receive a fresh cleansing, and purpose in your heart not to commit that act again. To put it a different way, as a Christian, you wouldn't want to take advantage of the grace afforded to you, but you would be motivated to strive for excellence (not perfection). You would purpose to cleanse yourself of the sin and not just roll around in the cesspool of life with no regard for holiness.

How do you demonstrate your appreciation for God's grace in your love relationship? Does your behavior toward your partner suggest you are truly committed to God? Do you take advantage of God's grace, or do you show a high regard for holiness? God's love for us was expensive. God's grace is free, but it is not cheap. If you have abused God's grace in the past, confess it, ask for His forgiveness, and pray that He will restore a passion to follow Him. You are always dependent on God's grace through Christ for your daily acceptance.

You will never be obedient enough to merit His favor. However, just because the essence of your relationship with God is grace doesn't mean you put obedience on the shelf. You still must struggle to fight the anti-God energy within you every day. Grace ultimately empowers you to resist temptation and frees you to persevere to the end.

FURTHER SCRIPTURAL MEDITATION
- Romans 6:14
- Titus 2:11–12
- Hebrews 10:26–29

Summarize, in your own words, the essence of this day's devotional on grace. Write down any thoughts, feelings, or insights in the space below.

My Father, I thank You that Your grace not only saves me, but it purifies me as well. Empower me today by Your Spirit to fight off the anti-God energy within me that resists Your continuing grace. Amen.

Serious Diagnosis

There is no difference, for all have sinned and fall short of the glory of God.

—ROMANS 3:22–23

*F*or a long time I (Ben) was in deep denial about my vision. For twenty-four years I had 20/20 vision, and I never imagined there would come a day when I would have to wear glasses or contacts. Then one day I was driving through the streets of Dallas with a friend who kept riding me because I couldn't make out the street names until I was five feet in front of them. She said, "Hey, Ben, have you ever thought about getting glasses?" I said, "You must be kidding. I have perfect vision."

Well, you can guess what happened next. I reluctantly made an eye appointment and discovered, much to my chagrin, that she was right. I desperately needed glasses. I had grossly misdiagnosed my condition.

For many years I held the same attitude concerning my spiritual condition before God. I didn't drink, smoke, dance, listen to rock music, or sleep around. I went to church, prayed, and read my Bible. About the wildest thing I ever did was smoke a few crayons (I didn't inhale) and get drunk on Kool-Aid at vacation Bible school. As I compared myself to other people both inside and outside the church, I concluded that I was a pretty good guy and that God must be really pleased by all of my good deeds. Boy, was I ever blind.

Over a long period of time, God revealed to me my true condition before Him. According to the Bible, there is no difference between the religious and the irreligious. It does not matter whether you are a missionary or a murderer, a preacher or a prostitute. We are all equally guilty and contaminated before God. We are sinners not only by choice but also by birth. We inherited this guilt and corruption from our original dysfunctional parent, Adam, when he disobeyed God and ate the forbidden fruit. We are natural-born sinners. There are no "good people" from God's perspective. We are born enemies of God, spiritually dead, and by nature deserving of God's wrath.

Just as I was in denial about my poor eyesight, I was in more serious denial about my spiritual condition. I never experienced God's grace until I realized the helplessness of my condition. And until we know the seriousness of our diagnosis, it is impossible to appreciate the cure. Unless we are willing to admit that we are sick, guilty, and separated from God, we will never experience the power of God's miraculous cure—grace.

The good news is that God has a prescription for our plight. His Rx for us is Jesus Christ. By condemning the human race through one man, Adam, God was then able to save those who received His grace through one man, Jesus Christ. Because of Adam's fatal decision, all were made sinners. Because of Christ's act of righteousness, His death in our place, all who trust in Him can be made righteous. Translation: we get to go to heaven because of what Jesus Christ did for us. That's why they call it amazing grace.

But wait—it doesn't stop there. God's grace initially gets us in the door of heaven, but we must rely upon this grace every day for a continual relationship with God. We need to be reminded of the value of God's grace because it alone gives us ongoing, intimate access to Him. Even on our most spiritual days, we are in desperate need of God's grace to be acceptable to Him. Embracing God's diagnosis and cure has radically changed my life forever. Let it change yours.

FURTHER SCRIPTURAL MEDITATION
- Romans 5:17–21
- Romans 8:1
- Ephesians 2:4–7

Summarize, in your own words, the essence of this day's devotional on grace. Write down any thoughts, feelings, or insights in the space below.

God, give me the humility to see myself as both a saint and a sinner. Teach me to stay humble as I grow in my relationship with You and others. Amen.

Amazing Grace

For it is by grace you have been saved, through faith—and this not from yourselves, it is the gift of God—not by works, so that no one can boast.

—EPHESIANS 2:8–9

It's Christmas Eve. You and your family have just finished a delicious meal of turkey, dressing, and sweet potatoes when suddenly you hear a knock at the door. You open the door and find a shivering elderly man standing on your holiday welcome mat. One glance at his tattered clothes and long beard tells you he has been living on the streets. He politely asks you for some food, and you run into the kitchen and return with a to-go plate of turkey and bread for him. The man thanks you and disappears into the night. Was your act of kindness a demonstration of grace? Some people define grace as giving someone something he does not deserve. From a human perspective what you did was a very kind act, but it falls short of illustrating true grace.

A picture of true grace would look like this: you have just finished eating this same holiday meal, and the same elderly man appears at your doorstep. He has a clear garbage bag draped over his shoulder filled with Christmas presents. Your jaw suddenly drops to your feet when you notice that the gifts in the bag are yours! Somehow he sneaked in a window and took all of your family Christmas presents, and now he has the nerve to beg you for food. So, you turn around and hurry to the kitchen and fix him a plate of food and send him on his way. That is true grace—giving someone the very opposite of what he deserves. No one in his right mind would do such an amazing act for a low-life Christmas thief.

From God's perspective we are all like this common criminal. We have stolen the goods from Him by choosing to break His commandments. The Bible says we are all sinners and fall short of God's standard of righteousness—that being 100 percent perfection. Because God is perfect and holy, He cannot look upon sin but must instead judge every act of disobedience as cosmic treason against His law. If God's requirement for acceptance is perfection, then how on earth can anybody pass the test? God's answer is Jesus Christ, the ultimate demonstration of true grace.

God became a man in the person of Jesus Christ. Jesus lived a perfect moral life. He always did what was right, and He never did anything wrong. He lived the perfect life that you or I could never live. He then died on the cross to pay the penalty for our sins with His very own blood. Christ was dead for three days, but on that third day He rose from the dead. The Bible tells us that on the cross, God treated Jesus Christ as if He had lived our lives so that He might treat us as if we had lived His life.

When you trust in Jesus Christ for your salvation, God declares you forgiven, not guilty. And it gets even better. He then transfers Christ's perfect life to your account so now you can be completely accepted in His sight. That is true grace.

We deserve God's wrath and punishment, but because of Christ's life and death in our place, we receive forgiveness and eternal life. We all stand before God with our clear garbage bag of stolen goods, but when we cry out to Him for grace through Jesus, He gives us freedom, forgiveness, and everlasting life— the very opposite of the things we deserve.

You should never grow weary of hearing the message of God's grace. A frustrated parishioner once asked Martin Luther why he preached the gospel of grace every Sunday. Luther replied, "Because every week you forget it." Today, reflect on God's provision of grace in your life. Thank Him for the reality that because of His grace, you are now fully acceptable in His sight and completely forgiven of all sin (past, present, and future). Now that's amazing!

FURTHER SCRIPTURAL MEDITATION
- 2 Corinthians 5:21–6:1
- Colossians 2:13–14
- Titus 3:4–7

Summarize, in your own words, the essence of this day's devotional on grace. Write down any thoughts, feelings, or insights in the space below.

Father, thank You that You have declared me perfectly acceptable and pleasing in Your sight because of the work of Jesus Christ for me. May I accept Your grace to strengthen and empower me to lead me home. Amen.

Focus

You then, my son, be strong in the grace that is in Christ Jesus.

—2 TIMOTHY 2:1

When I (Ben) was a little boy, I used to daydream about winning a gold medal in the Olympic Games. I didn't know whether the gold would be in swimming, track, or skiing. I just knew that I had to experience the ultimate high of being the best in the world at some sport. Somewhere along life's path, I stopped dreaming about becoming an Olympian, but I must confess that whenever the Games are on, I am glued to the TV set.

Having watched the Olympics for many years now, I have seen reporters interview myriads of gold medal–winning athletes, from tough Greco-Roman wrestlers to petite ice-skaters. The questions often sound somewhat like these: "How did you do it? Why didn't you choke under pressure? How did you endure the grueling months of training?" Millions of viewers around the globe wait eagerly on the edge of their seats to hear the same refrain: "Focus." "When I felt the heat, I just stayed focused on my form" or, "If I got depressed or burned out during my preparation for the Games, I would force myself to stay focused on the goal."

Any individual, corporation, or church that is making an impact on the world has mastered the art of maintaining laser focus on what really matters. Can you imagine what would happen if you truly focused on the task at hand this week at work? Or what if you focused all your free time on becoming a better communicator in your relationships? The discipline of focus allows you to harness the power of your potential.

One of the greatest leaders in the history of the world was a man named Paul of Tarsus. He was a highly educated and highly motivated convert to Christianity in the first century. If you could extend a microphone to heaven and interview Paul about how he was able to endure ridicule, persecution, beatings, imprisonments, and ultimately death, he would most likely say, "I stayed focused on grace." Shortly before his martyrdom in Rome, he penned the words "be strong in the grace that is in Christ Jesus" to his young disciple Timothy. He pleaded with this future leader, "If you want your life to have maximum impact, if you truly want to make a difference for God in this brief stay here on earth, then focus like a laser on the grace of God."

For the past fourteen years, God has been opening my eyes to His amazing grace. And I guarantee you that if you will focus on this same grace, your life will continue to change, and your relationships will be enhanced. Grace will transform the way you experience God. Grace will give you compassion toward others. Grace will modify the way you see yourself. Grace will take you off the performance treadmill and free you up to walk in the love and acceptance of God through Jesus Christ.

Focus on grace today and every day this week. Ask God to help you appreciate the richness of His grace to you and how it can transform your life from the inside out.

FURTHER SCRIPTURAL MEDITATION
- John 1:17
- Acts 20:32
- Romans 5:1–2

Summarize, in your own words, the essence of this day's devotional on grace. Write down any thoughts, feelings, or insights in the space below.

Dear Lord, help me to cultivate an attitude of gratitude for everything You do in my life. Help me to stay focused not on my performance but on the grace given to me through Jesus Christ. Amen.

Dear Father,

I come into Your presence today in the name of Jesus Christ. Because of His death and resurrection, I can call You Father. I know You have adopted me into Your family, and I am so grateful that You have provided a way for me to know You.

Dear God, for such a long time, I have tried to earn Your favor by obeying all the rules. I thought that all of my religious duties and so-called righteous deeds would make You love me more. Thank You for opening my eyes to the fact that it is only through Your grace that I am accepted into Your family, and only by Your grace that I remain in Your family from day to day. Help me to continue to rely on Your grace on my worst days and my best days. Keep me from going back to look at my works as a means to earning Your blessings in my life.

I thank You for the cross of Jesus Christ. Thank You for the forgiveness and righteousness that flow to me through the death of Christ. May I never boast in my goodness or spirituality, but may I boast only in what Christ has done for me.

In Jesus' name I pray. Amen.

Prayer Journal

PRAISE (ADORATION):

REPENTANCE (CONFESSION):

APPRECIATION (THANKSGIVING):

YIELD (REQUESTS):

A Foundation of Grace

Today we would like to encourage you and your partner to set aside some time just for the two of you. Perhaps you can go to lunch, drive to the park, or get away to some other setting that might be conducive to discussing the topic of *grace*. Keep in mind that the purpose is to ask questions, listen with compassion, and share with each other about your experience regarding the issue for this past week. This is a time to listen and seek to understand each other with a spirit of support and encouragement. Ultimately this venture together is intended to build a stronger foundation of spiritual intimacy.

Grace is one of those words that sounds as good as it is. It flows off the lips and just automatically seems to have a comforting quality about it. We've looked at grace this past week and discovered that it is indeed as good as it sounds. Grace is God's answer to a lost world; an undeserved gift that provides us with salvation and assures us of an eternal relationship with almighty God. You've learned this week that no matter how "good" we try to be, we all stand guilty before a holy God, and without grace we have no basis for a relationship with Him. You've come to appreciate that God's grace is free, but it isn't cheap. Because of His grace, we are motivated toward a holy and pure lifestyle. And you've learned that you are not to be burdened by your daily performance, but you are to live life in freedom based upon God's grace.

QUESTIONS FOR DISCUSSION

1. What have you discovered to be most meaningful concerning the subject of God's grace?

2. Have you found yourself living life based upon the performance trap?

3. Discuss with your partner how he or she might encourage you to live life with a perspective of grace.

4. Talk to each other about the difference between cheap grace and free grace.

5. How can your partner inspire you to maintain focus on grace instead of works?

Sunday

Sermon Notes:

Insights to Share:

Prayer

Next to the wonder of seeing my Savior will be,
I think, the wonder that I made so little use of the power of prayer.

—D. L. MOODY

Mind how you pray. Make real business of it. Let it never be a dead formality.

—CHARLES SPURGEON

Prayer doesn't change God, but it changes him who prays.

—SØREN KIERKEGAARD

The less I pray, the harder it gets. The more I pray, the better it goes.

—MARTIN LUTHER

To Whom Are You Praying?

If you, then, though you are evil, know how to give good gifts to your children, how much more will your Father in heaven give good gifts to those who ask him!

—MATTHEW 7:11

"I am an atheist," Josh declared. After several weeks into what began as relationship counseling, I (Sam) had asked Josh to tell me about his faith. He went on to defend his doubts of a loving and sovereign God based on intellectual differences, evolution, the Resurrection, and global pain and suffering. I eventually asked him to tell me about his family history. I was not surprised to learn that his father had left his mom and him when Josh was quite young, and he had since remarried two other times.

I certainly felt his pain, and yet I had to be honest with him: "Your problem with God is not intellectual. It's really that you have projected the character of your earthly father onto your heavenly Father, who is nothing like the man who left you and your mother."

A. W. Tozer once observed, "The most important thing about you is what you think about God." In light of this principle, we suggest that your ability to understand and embrace the truth about God (His identity and character) has the greatest impact upon who you are and how you live life. Many of us carry around childish conceptions of God, even though we may have deep faith and strong commitment. However, the power of prayer hinges upon your understanding of who God is.

To whom are you praying? What is your view of God? Do you see Him as a passive or distant elderly man lurking somewhere in the outer cosmos? Do you fear that He is uninvolved or unconcerned about your life? Maybe your concept of God is like that of a stern policeman in the sky whose sole purpose is to punish you when you do wrong. Or perhaps you assume He is no more than a casual friend.

The Scriptures present a God who is intimately involved and concerned with every detail of your life. He is a loving heavenly Father who longs for a close, personal relationship with you. In fact, Jesus was the first person to suggest that God was like a Father. He explicitly gives us permission to address God as "our Father" (in the Lord's Prayer) and approach Him in that manner. Of course, Scripture also indicates that God is a sovereign King; therefore, we also must approach Him with a sense of awe, humility, and reverence.

If you could reduce prayer to its most basic level, you would discover that it is simply a process of communication with your heavenly Father. It's difficult to imagine how anyone could have open, free-flowing dialogue with God without a proper understanding of who He really is.

We challenge you to consider your view of God. You may

know God as Father from an intellectual standpoint, but how do you experience Him when you approach His throne in prayer? What is your true conception of Him? Make sure you seek to maintain a biblical understanding of God and approach Him with a balanced view: heavenly Father and holy King. Take time now to thank God for the privilege of having an intimate relationship with Him and the confidence that you may approach His almighty throne with the boldness of a trusting child.

FURTHER SCRIPTURAL MEDITATION
- Isaiah 6:1–5
- Matthew 6:8–13
- Romans 11:22

Summarize, in your own words, the essence of this day's devotional on prayer. Write down any thoughts, feelings, or insights in the space below.

Heavenly Father, thank You for the gift of prayer, for the wonderful opportunity to access Your throne at any time. Help me to commit my life to daily prayer with You. Amen.

The Ultimate Purpose of Prayer

*Father, if you are willing, take this cup from me; yet not my will, but
yours be done.*

—LUKE 22:42

Not too long ago, Academy Award winner Anthony
Hopkins portrayed the life of Oxford professor and theologian
C. S. Lewis in one of my favorite movies, *Shadowlands*. It is a
gripping story about Lewis's awakening to the harsh realities of
passionate love and the nature of suffering. In one scene, as his
wife is dying of cancer, his intellectual friend from Oxford flip-
pantly encourages him to pray for her recovery. Lewis chides
him with his classic response: "I pray because I can't help
myself; I pray because I'm helpless. The need flows out of me
all the time—waking and sleeping. Prayer doesn't change God; it
changes me." In other words, this great man of the faith wasn't
praying because he suddenly found himself in crisis. He was
always in prayer anyway, and he understood that his primary
motivation for prayer was not to manipulate God but to bring
about a transformation in his own heart.

As a form of spiritual connection with God, prayer represents
many things, including having intimacy with Him, seeking

clarification for the direction in our lives from Him, and petitioning for our needs to be met by Him. But let's be clear. A primary purpose of prayer is not to change God's mind or get something from Him like the proverbial genie in the bottle. Prayer isn't a hocus-pocus process whereby we say the "magic words" with enough faith and then God will grant our wish. To the contrary, prayer is an ongoing process of communication, which enables us to become more like Christ and discover God's desires for our lives.

Please don't misunderstand. That's not to say that our prayers don't have an impact on others. We are in joint cooperation with God as the agents of change in the world around us. But prayer is ultimately about changing our hearts.

In his book *Celebration of Discipline*, Richard Foster writes, "Prayer is the central avenue God uses to transform us . . . The closer we come to the heartbeat of God, the more we desire to be conformed to Christ." Isn't that a wonderful way to put prayer in proper perspective? Have you ever thought about prayer in those terms? Meditate on the significance of this ultimate purpose of prayer; consider this notion that it's more about changing you and changing your heart than it is about trying to manipulate God to conform to your will. As you continue through this devotional, begin to pray with anticipation that God is working on you to strengthen your faith, character, and heart.

FURTHER SCRIPTURAL MEDITATION
- Matthew 26:39, 42

- 2 Corinthians 12:7–10
- 1 John 5:14

Summarize, in your own words, the essence of this day's devotional on prayer. Write down any thoughts, feelings, or insights in the space below.

Lord, I acknowledge that my motives for prayer aren't always clean. I ask that You would change me and change my heart through the discipline of prayer. Amen.

Authentic Prayer

When you pray, do not keep on babbling like pagans, for they think they will be heard because of their many words.

—Matthew 6:7

Daniel walked into my (Ben's) office for a counseling session wearing a dark Hickey-Freeman suit, starched white shirt, blue silk tie, and Rolex watch. This guy was sharp and polished. He even brought typed notes of an outline to help him convey his reason for the appointment. During our first session together, it was apparent that I was getting the "best foot forward" version from Daniel. He was there to impress me; to tell me things that he thought I wanted to hear. His mask was on, his facade was up, his defenses were high, and we had a "wonderful" time chatting about all the superficial things in life that had absolutely nothing to do with his reason for being in counseling. It took us weeks to penetrate the surface layers and tap into the real hurt and pain associated with the loss of his family. But that's when the real work began. Most people enter the counseling office in a similar fashion, completely unaware of their defensive presentation.

Unfortunately we often do the same thing with God. When

we go to Him in prayer, we tend to approach Him with an overly favorable presentation of ourselves and tell Him what we think He wants to hear. We often mistake prayer for some ritualized, formal discourse sprinkled with a handful of "religious" pleasantries. I don't know about you, but sometimes I feel that I must get my act together first before I can present myself to God. Doing this never works and inevitably only serves as a barrier toward intimacy with Him. In truth, we need to come to God "as is."

Prayer is getting honest and real with God. Jesus stated that our prayers should be simple, honest, and direct ("do not keep on babbling like pagans"). Prayer is taking off the masks and letting down the defenses. The psalmists clearly demonstrated that kind of raw, passionate expression to God. True prayer takes place when we are authentic in His presence and we speak from the depth of our hearts. It's finding the quiet solitude where we are free to express our joys, longings, and dreams as well as our greatest fears, concerns, and disappointments. This communion with God produces true intimacy with Him.

Jesus said,

Here's what I want you to do: Find a quiet, secluded place so you won't be tempted to role-play before God. Just be there as simply and honestly as you can manage. The focus will shift from you to God, and you will begin to sense his grace.

The world is full of so-called prayer warriors who are prayer-ignorant. They're full of formulas and programs and advice, peddling techniques for getting what you want from God. Don't fall for that nonsense. This is your Father you are dealing with, and He knows better than you what you need. (Matt. 6:6–8 *The Message*)

To maintain this level of authenticity and transparency, we must be in daily contact with Him. Of course, Jesus was our supreme model for prayer by example. We read in Mark 1:35, "Very early in the morning, while it was still dark, Jesus got up, left the house and went off to a solitary place, where he prayed." The Scriptures also reveal that He often withdrew from the crowds and went to a "lonely place" to pray. We see this after His baptism when He retreated to the desert for forty days; on the Mount of Olives; after the miracle of the feeding of the five thousand; and in the Garden of Gethsemane before He was to be crucified. We get the impression that Christ spent time alone every single day in spite of all the demands He had to fulfill.

Now let's get this straight. If Jesus Christ, the second person of the Trinity, needed time alone with the Father, how much more do you and I need to commit to this time of solitude for daily spiritual renewal?

FURTHER SCRIPTURAL MEDITATION

- Psalm 119:57–58
- Romans 8:26–27
- Philippians 4:6–7

Summarize, in your own words, the essence of this day's devotional on prayer. Write down any thoughts, feelings, or insights in the space below.

Dear God, give me a strong desire for quiet solitude with You. Father, help me to learn how to be real and authentic in Your presence. Amen.

Prayer Is Listening

I am the good shepherd; I know my sheep and my sheep know me . . .
The watchman opens the gate for him, and the sheep listen to his voice.
He calls his own sheep by name and leads them out. When he has
brought out all his own, he goes on ahead of them.

—JOHN 10:14, 3–4

These survey results just in: when people pray, they spend 99.9 percent of their time talking to God, and they reserve the other 0.1 percent for listening. I think it's safe to assume that most of us approach God with a wish list and a definite agenda. We are more interested in telling Him what we need and what He should do than we are in truly seeking His direction for our lives: "Lord, bless me. Lord, help me. Lord, give me . . . Lord, bail me out just this one last time." Can you relate?

Effective communication takes place when the message received by the listener reflects the intent of the speaker. It stands to reason that if prayer is simply communication with God and effective communication is a two-way process, then prayer must also include an element of *listening* to God.

Admittedly this is a hard one to wrap our minds around

because we cannot see God in the physical realm, and He does not typically speak to us with an audible voice. And yet one of the clear themes of the Bible indicates that God actively talks to His people. Therefore, we must assume that He does not hide Himself or His will from you and me.

If you make yourself available and you genuinely desire to know His will, then you can hear His voice. Listening with your spiritual ears is just as important as sharing your heart. Remember, God already knows what you are thinking and feeling. He knows what you need before you even ask! It stands to reason that you would benefit greatly from listening to Him.

We love the metaphorical language of Jesus recorded in the gospel of John regarding the shepherd and his sheep. By nature, sheep tend to be timid, easily influenced, defenseless, and just plain stupid animals. For our purposes the most relevant lesson we can derive from this passage of Scripture includes our sense of helplessness and desperate need to be led by God every step of the way. Ah, but we must listen to His voice.

Honestly I'm afraid to let even one day go by without attempting to hear God's voice and seek His direction. And it goes without saying that all of my major decisions in life are preceded by earnest prayer and active listening to God. Even though I am a new creation and I have a new heart, at times I still find myself leaning toward my selfish (and foolish) ambitions. Hence, I'm on my knees (often quite literally) every day to ensure that I may continue to walk in the Spirit and hear His voice.

So how does God speak to us? Primarily through Scripture. Sometimes it's quite subtle—a whisper in your spirit or perhaps a verse of Scripture may come to mind. At other times words from the Bible will suddenly leap off the page and have direct personal application. Regardless of the method God uses to speak to you, we challenge you to make sure to run everything through the grid of Scripture. Determine that what He seems to be telling you is consistent with His revealed, written Word. The psalmist declared, "Your word is a lamp to my feet and a light for my path" (Ps. 119:105).

If you haven't already done so, we encourage you to add a whole new dimension to your spiritual life and begin the process of two-way dialogue with God. In other words, allow Him the opportunity to speak to you for a change! Of course, it's hard to avoid the parallel principle in your romantic relationship. So much of true intimacy and closeness relies upon your ability to listen effectively to your partner.

Make a commitment today to be a conscientious listener in all your relationships. Most important, establish the practice of listening to God with your heart. He's waiting for the opportunity to speak to you, so let Him. You should be pleasantly surprised!

FURTHER SCRIPTURAL MEDITATION
- Psalm 66:19–20
- Jeremiah 29:11–13
- Jeremiah 33:3

Summarize, in your own words, the essence of this day's devotional on prayer. Write down any thoughts, feelings, or insights in the space below.

Lord, I trust that You do, indeed, speak to us in a very real way. Help me to develop the habit of listening to You, and teach me to discern Your voice from my own. Amen.

Pray Without Ceasing

Be joyful always; pray continually; give thanks in all circumstances,
for this is God's will for you in Christ Jesus.

— 1 THESSALONIANS 5:16–18

When it comes to prayer, there are at least two forms of communion with God. One is a more deliberate, specific time away from the daily grind in a private prayer closet. You are essentially devoted to one thing—communicating with God without any external distractions.

But there is another form of prayer. It involves living your life with a spirit of continual exchange—an ongoing conversation with God throughout the day. In 1 Thessalonians 5, Paul encouraged the people of Thessalonica to "pray continually," or more literally, to "pray without ceasing." This is not just some pious platitude to file away for a rainy day when you've got a case of the blues. Paul was giving specific instruction for daily, moment-by-moment living. He even appealed to an ultimate authority by saying that this kind of prayer is God's will.

Some call this *practicing the presence* of God. Note the term "practicing," which implies that this process is unnatural. We force ourselves to do this until it becomes a habit. So what does this look like? Henri Nouwen explains, "To pray . . . means to think and live in the presence of God. All our actions must have their origin in prayer. Praying is not an isolated activity; it takes place in the midst of all the things and affairs that keep us active." This applies in all circumstances: driving to work each morning, interacting with others on a social level, attending meetings, listening to a lecture, working out, or even engaging in an in-depth conversation with a close friend.

At any given moment of the day, you hold a conversation with yourself somewhere in the back regions of your mind. What we're suggesting is that you turn this conversation into prayer as you maintain at least some awareness that God is compassionately standing with you at all times. Billy Graham has often said that during conversation with others, he is simultaneously praying to God to give him the words to best communicate God's truth for each moment.

The benefits of praying continually are innumerable. To start with, when you practice the presence of God (literally when you live each moment with the understanding that God's Spirit is in your midst), you are empowered by His Spirit. You experience an inner peace and a confidence that come only from God. Furthermore, this process creates a whole different outlook on life. Even mundane tasks and seemingly superficial interactions with others become divine appointments ordained by God with grand purpose and meaning. This process gives you an eternal perspective—a God's-eye view of things.

You may initially view this kind of prayer as an immense and time-consuming burden. However, consider what Dallas

Willard says in his book *The Spirit of the Disciplines:* "Constant prayer will only 'burden' us as wings burden the bird in flight." In other words, living each moment of the day with an attitude of prayer strengthens you and allows you to soar above the mundane and see things from God's perspective.

We challenge you, starting today, to begin to practice the presence of God. Experiment with this form of moment-by-moment living. We think you'll be blessed. But don't take our word for it. See for yourself!

FURTHER SCRIPTURAL MEDITATION
- Matthew 28:18–20
- Luke 18:1–8
- Philippians 4:6–7

Summarize, in your own words, the essence of this day's devotional on prayer. Write down any thoughts, feelings, or insights in the space below.

Dear God, thank You for the privilege of 24–hour-a-day access to You. Help me to learn the art of ongoing dialogue with You throughout each day. Amen.

Dear Lord,

I thank You that we have access to You through our relationship with Jesus Christ. Thank You that I can come to You about everything and You always hear my prayer. I praise You that You are a holy King and a loving Father. Teach me to come to You as my holy King out of humility and reverence, knowing that You are all-powerful and able to do all things. I also want to see You as my loving Father, who cares for me and all that I go through and wants me to consider Him in all of my life.

Help me to come to You in everything, not just my wants and needs but also with my everyday decisions and choices, with my mind and my heart. Forgive me that I often pray to change Your will or get something from You instead of praying to change my will to match Yours.

I want to become more like Jesus in my thoughts, words, and deeds, but I will need Your help every day to make progress. Help me to grow in my prayer life with You. Lord, I want to learn how to pray continually and to listen to You better through spending more time in prayer and in Your Word.

In Jesus' name I pray. Amen.

Prayer Journal

PRAISE (ADORATION):

REPENTANCE (CONFESSION):

APPRECIATION (THANKSGIVING):

YIELD (REQUESTS):

A Foundation of Prayer

$\mathscr{T}$oday we challenge you and your partner to set aside some time just for the two of you. We encourage you to find a peaceful setting to discuss the topic of *prayer*. Keep in mind that the purpose is to ask questions, listen with compassion, and share with each other about your experiences regarding the issue for this past week. This is not a time to debate or argue about theological perspectives. It is a time to listen and seek to understand each other with a spirit of support and encouragement. Ultimately this venture together is intended to build a stronger foundation of spiritual intimacy.

This past week we have addressed the subject of prayer. You have learned that prayer is the primary method we use to connect with God. You have discovered that prayer doesn't necessarily come naturally; it requires a deliberate effort, some degree of intentional planning, and at least some kind of structure. You have also learned that prayer is a process of allowing yourself to be authentic in God's presence, and it is primarily His vehicle for changing you, changing your heart.

We want you to take this time to discuss the discipline of prayer. However, we would caution you about trying to pray together at this point unless you are engaged to be married or in the later stage of your relationship. Because prayer can be one of the most intimate forms of connection, we want you to have a solid foundation of friendship and emotional connection before you introduce this component to the relationship.

QUESTIONS FOR DISCUSSION

1. How would you evaluate your prayer life? Do you begin and end each day with prayer? Do you pray continually throughout the day? Share your answers with each other.

2. Everyone struggles with the discipline of prayer. It's a universal experience. Discuss your difficulties with prayer. What are the barriers and hindrances you seem to encounter?

3. How would you assess your ability to be authentic and real before the God of the universe?

4. Talk to each other about your view of God. Do you see Him as an angry older man in the sky? Do you view Him as a passive, distant grandfather in the outer cosmos? Or are you able to approach Him as He really is—a loving heavenly Father who is intimately involved and concerned about every detail of your life? Discuss your views.

5. How can you pray for each other? Do you share your prayer needs?

6. Have you committed this relationship to prayer? Have you asked God to show you how you can serve Him together? Have you asked God about what may be lacking, harmful, or unhealthy in your relationship? Talk to each other about how you might use the discipline of prayer to enhance the relationship.

7. Praying together is one of the greatest catalysts for intimacy in marriage. Would you and your partner be willing to start praying together as a couple? Discuss whether you are ready for this level of commitment.

SUNDAY

(TODAY'S DATE)

SERMON NOTES:

INSIGHTS TO SHARE:

The Word

As the soul is dyed by the thoughts,
let no day pass without contact with
the best literature of the world.

—WILLIAM OSLER

The highest of all is not to understand the highest but to act upon it.

—SØREN KIERKEGAARD

The Bible vindicates itself because it is such excellent medicine.
It has never failed to cure a single patient if
only he took his prescription honestly.

—DR. HOWARD ATWOOD KELLY

Upstream Against the Current

Do not conform any longer to the pattern of this world, but be transformed by the renewing of your mind.

—ROMANS 12:2

Many moons ago, I (Ben) canoed down the Guadalupe River with my good friend Jay Stovall. It was our first time to ever tackle a river, so we were thrilled to take on this new challenge. Jay and I had a relatively smooth ride downstream until we hit our first set of serious rapids. I was at the front of the boat, and he was steering from the back. For some unknown reason, Jay decided to stand up as we shot the white water, and our canoe capsized. Fortunately we did not drown, and we were able to recover the boat and paddles. My friend lost his T-shirt, and I cut my knee open. I still have a small scar on my left knee to remind me of that infamous trip on the Guadalupe.

Life is like a river. Most of us just jump into the river of life and allow the current to slowly (or sometimes swiftly) pull us downstream. When you are in a river, you don't ever see the current, but you know it's always there. The current system of this world is constantly influencing and controlling the course of your life on a daily basis, and you don't even realize it. You are being controlled by current events, current views, current fears, and current challenges.

A recent study revealed that 98 percent of Americans own a television and the average TV set is on seven hours a day. Another poll showed that 48 percent of evangelical Christians rely on newspapers and TV reports for their main source of truth, while only 5 percent look to religious leaders for the same. You cannot afford to simply go with the flow of your culture and allow it to dash your life on the rocks.

Today's verse encourages you to confront the world's system by the renewing of your mind in the truth of the Word of God. If you are not regularly consulting God's Word for truth and direction, you will not succeed in God's eyes. The world system is empowered by the three *i*'s: *increase* your possessions, *impress* others, and *indulge* yourself. In contrast, God's Word says you should love Him with all your heart, soul, mind, and body, and love other people as much as you love yourself. God calls you to turn from selfishness and start serving others. You should give to those in need, find your acceptance in Christ, and practice self-control. You can't go upstream against the current unless you are daily renewing your mind with Scripture and trusting in the power of the Spirit to energize you to do God's will.

Take an inventory of your life and consider whether the world's system is drifting your life off course. Make sure that you are firmly positioned in the lifeboat of God's Word and that you seek to apply His timeless truths. And yield to the power of the Holy Spirit to propel you upstream against the current.

FURTHER SCRIPTURAL MEDITATION
- Psalm 1:1–2
- Psalm 119:97–105
- John 8:31–32

Summarize, in your own words, the essence of this day's devotional on God's Word. Write down any thoughts, feelings, or insights in the space below.

Dear God, show me the areas in my life where I am merely going with the flow contrary to Your Word. Help me to turn from these sins and pursue Your course for my life. Amen.

God's Will

This is God's will for you in Christ Jesus.

—1 THESSALONIANS 5:18

*D*o you struggle with finding God's will for your life? Whom does He want you to marry? What job does He want you to take? Where does He want you to live?

Years ago I was faced with a difficult decision that had both temporal and eternal consequences. I had to discern the will of God on that life-or-death decision. I had two options. If I chose Plan A, God definitely could have blessed me. But if I chose Plan A and God really wanted me to choose Plan B, then I could have been totally out of His will. There were no Scriptures that related to the decision, so I was forced to listen to the inner voice of the Spirit.

As I listened, I heard that voice say to me, *Eat at Wendy's.* You see, I was torn between eating at Wendy's or McDonald's; I didn't want to miss His leading and eat at the wrong place. My understanding of how to discover the will of God for my life was a little off base at the time. I needed a big McDose of sound teaching on the issue.

Discerning God's will is not always easy, but let me share

with you a statement that may help: *God's will for your life is found in God's Word*. You could solve most of your problems with trying to hear God's voice and discern His leadings by opening up the Bible and reading it on a daily basis. You see, our hang-ups with this whole issue arise from a misunderstanding of the will of God.

God has two wills. The first will is God's sovereign, predetermined will that will be accomplished no matter what. Nothing can stop the awesome plan of God, and it will be carried out in His timing and in His manner. Period. This first will is also called His secret will. God's second will is called His moral will. This will is clearly revealed to us in the sixty-six books of the Bible. It contains promises, commands, warnings, and provisions to sufficiently guide us in this life. God's secret will is known only to Him, hence, the word *secret*. God's moral will is known to all through the Scriptures. The problem occurs when we want to sneak a peek at God's secret will before it has been revealed. Often we are too concerned with trying to anticipate His next move.

The bottom line is this: don't worry about God's secret, predetermined will. Just trust that God is going to work out His plan for your life as He guides you providentially and focus on obeying God's moral will day by day by day. When you recognize your dependence upon God for holiness, and you humbly seek to live your life according to His guidelines and moral teachings, you will be in the middle of His will for your life.

God's will for your life is more relational (love God and others) than it is geographical (know where to live) or occupational (recognize what job to take). His will for you today is for you to love Him with all your heart, mind, body, and soul, and to love others as much as you love yourself. God's will is also for you to follow the desires of your heart within the bounds of His moral prescriptions. Saint Augustine said it best: "Love God and do whatever you want."

FURTHER SCRIPTURAL MEDITATION
- Deuteronomy 29:29
- Ephesians 1:4–5
- 1 Thessalonians 4:3–8

Summarize, in your own words, the essence of this day's devotional on God's Word. Write down any thoughts, feelings, or insights in the space below.

Father, I accept that Your will for me is that I would immerse myself in Your Word. Teach me to obey Your commands in Scripture, to love You, and to love others. Amen.

Self-Talk

As he thinketh in his heart, so is he.

—PROVERBS 23:7 KJV

*O*ne of the things I (Ben) am least proud of is the mess associated with my freshman dorm room. The level of filth and
grime was unimaginable. The sink was dark brown from my
roommate emptying out his "spit cups" used while chewing
tobacco. There were old Domino's Pizza boxes, McDonald's
wrappers, and wadded-up papers covering the floor. We never
changed our sheets, so there were Coke stains and dirt from
our shoes. On Parents Weekend, I went down the hall to take
a shower, and when I returned ten minutes later, a group of
moms and dads had swarmed around the door of our room.
They were laughing and motioning to other parents to take a
look at how disgustingly messy our domicile had become.

Your mind can get just as cluttered and filthy as my old dorm
room. When you fail to confess your sins to God on a regular
basis, and when you are reluctant to deal with self-condemning
thoughts that come from the devil, your mind becomes a most
unsanitary place. Many times you can fall into a spiritual rut or
malaise because you don't practice healthy self-talk.

A revolutionary "discovery" in the field of psychology is the basic idea that our thoughts and attitudes create our moods. In other words, external events cannot make us feel anything; rather, our beliefs about these circumstances affect how we will feel. Self-talk is everything.

Of course, God already knew this and wrote about this principle centuries ago. The book of Proverbs warns of the importance of our self-talk. Likewise, 2 Corinthians encourages us to "take captive every thought to make it obedient to Christ" (10:5). The book of Romans also instructs us to be transformed by the renewing of our minds. The point is clear: you have a responsibility to think about what is uplifting, right, pure, healthy, and encouraging, and most of all to think on what is true.

Dr. D. Martyn Lloyd-Jones was a prominent physician before he became one of the most renowned preachers of the twentieth century. He had a lot to say about mind maintenance and how we must talk to ourselves with the Word of God:

I say that we must talk to ourselves instead of allowing "ourselves" to talk to us! Do you realize what this means? I suggest that the main trouble in this whole matter of spiritual depression in a sense is this, that we allow our self to talk to us instead of talking to our self. Am I just trying to be deliberately paradoxical? Have you realized that most of your unhappiness in life is due to the fact that you are listening to yourself instead of talking to yourself? Take those thoughts that come to you the moment you wake up in the morning.

You have not originated them, but they start talking to you, they bring back the problems of yesterday, etc. Somebody is talking. Who is talking to you? Your self is talking to you. Now [the psalmist's] treatment was this; instead of allowing this self to talk to him, he starts talking to himself. "Why art thou cast down, O my soul?" he asks. His soul had been depressing him, crushing him. So he stands up and says: "Self, listen for a moment, I will speak to you . . . Why art thou cast down?—What business have you to be disquieted?" . . . And then you must go on to remind yourself of God, Who He is, and what God is and what God has done, and what God pledged Himself to do. Then having done that, end on this great note: defy yourself, and defy other people, and defy the devil and the whole world, and say with this man: "I shall praise Him for the help of His countenance."

What a powerful concept! Speak to yourself instead of allowing your condemning and worrying self to speak to you. Try that out today. Clean up the dorm room of your mind. Practice healthy self-talk by preaching the truth of God's love, power, and presence to yourself when you experience guilt or depression. He is with you always. He loves you so much that He sent His Son to die in your place.

"As he thinketh in his heart, so is he." Think God's thoughts to yourself as you go throughout your day and you will have a clear mind.

FURTHER SCRIPTURAL MEDITATION
- Romans 12:2
- 2 Corinthians 10:4–5
- Philippians 4:8

Summarize, in your own words, the essence of this day's devotional on God's Word. Write down any thoughts, feelings, or insights in the space below.

Lord, keep me focused on the truth of Your Word rather than what my feelings communicate to me. May I renew my mind on Your truth that I am a beloved child of the Father. Amen.

Temptation

Jesus answered, "It is written: 'Man does not live on bread alone, but on every word that comes from the mouth of God.'"

—MATTHEW 4:4

*T*emptation is a universal struggle. Centuries ago a group of religious men came up with a new way to combat sexual temptation. Whenever they saw an attractive woman on the street, they immediately closed their eyes and walked in a different direction. Naturally the well-intentioned men were constantly running into walls, columns, and poles and eventually became known as the "Bloody Nosed Pharisees." You must admire their motive, even though their method was less than perfect.

Everyone is tempted by something or someone on a daily basis. Some are tempted to lust; others are tempted to shop, eat, or drink excessively; and still others are tempted to cheat. Temptation is something that you must deal with every single day, and if you continually give in to temptation, you will reap the negative and disastrous consequences as a result.

Jesus dealt with temptation by harnessing the power of three simple, yet profound words. In Matthew 4, Satan tempted Jesus three times, and every time Christ responded with three words: "It is written." Say those words out loud: "It is written." Jesus used those three words to introduce the truth and expose the lies from Satan: "It is written: 'Man does not live on bread alone, but on every word that comes from the mouth of God'"; and "It is also written: 'Do not put the Lord your God to the test'"; and "It is written: 'Worship the Lord your God and serve him only.'"

It is clear that Jesus had been feeding on God's Word throughout His entire life. He had made it a habit to renew His mind on the truth revealed in the Scriptures. There is no doubt that Christ spent hours praying over, meditating on, and memorizing the law of God. When temptation flew into town, Christ was ready to defend Himself with the truth from God's Word.

To have victory over the things that continually tempt you, start memorizing the Word of God. One way to begin is to write on a small note card some Bible verses related to your specific area of temptation. Place the card in your shirt pocket or purse, and throughout the day, pull it out and read it to yourself. You may even want to read it aloud (but make sure you are alone or you might lose your friends or your job). Make copies of the card and tape them on the mirror in your bathroom, on your fridge, or on the dashboard of your car. Doing this will keep the truth of God in front of you at all times. Another method you can use is to read the verse or verses into a tape recorder and play them back on your way to work. You might even include the words "it is written" to remind yourself that you are quoting the very Word of God.

Don't condemn yourself for being tempted. Being tempted with sinful thoughts or desires is not a sin but acting on them is. Discover the amazing power to resist temptation by using the very words of God.

FURTHER SCRIPTURAL MEDITATION

- Psalm 119:11
- Matthew 4:1–11
- Hebrews 4:12

Summarize, in your own words, the essence of this day's devotional on God's Word. Write down any thoughts, feelings, or insights in the space below.

Dear God, teach me to nourish myself on Your Holy Word that I might be strong in the fight of faith. Help me to meditate on Your Word to resist temptation in my life. Amen.

Just Do It

Do not merely listen to the word, and so deceive yourselves. Do what it says.

—JAMES 1:22

$\mathscr{M}$ike loves to scuba dive. He bought a 1,500-page book titled *Everything You Need to Know About Diving* at Sportsmart. Every day at 6:00 A.M. Mike picks up the scuba book from his bedside table and devours it. He always reads with a pen in hand, so when he spots a sentence or paragraph that is really illuminating, he will underline it or put a star by it in the margin. On Thursday nights, Mike gathers with a group of friends at his apartment to discuss everything they have been learning about scuba diving. On Sundays, they put on wet suits, diving masks, and oxygen tanks, and they head down to the beach. They love to watch the surfers ride the waves, and they especially enjoy watching the fishermen, who wade out into the water to catch fish.

If you approached Mike sitting on the beach with his buddies and asked, "Do you ever go scuba diving?" he might answer, "Of course. I go scuba diving every day right here in this book, *Everything You Need to Know About Diving*. And on

Thursdays, we gather at my house to talk about the insights we've learned that week. And we also hang out here near the water every Sunday to get a closer look at the beauty of the ocean."

How many Christians do you know who are just like Mike? They read the Bible every day, huddle in a small group during the week, and put on their Sunday best to go to church. They know a lot about the Bible from reading it and hanging out with other believers, but there is no difference in the way they live. The book of James encourages you to put your faith to work.

Too many people sit and listen to the Word of God every week, but do nothing about it. Faith without works is no faith at all. It is dead. James said, "Don't merely hear the Word of God, but do what God is telling you to do."

God gives Christian singles a crystal-clear commandment in 2 Corinthians 6:14: "Do not be yoked together with unbe-lievers." In 1 Corinthians 7, He tells singles they are free to marry anyone they wish as long as the person is in Christ. The Bible gives no wiggle room for dating or marrying someone who is outside the faith.

So how can you discern whether someone is a true follower of Christ? The sure sign of a true believer is someone who talks the talk *and* walks the walk; the works match the faith. Some-one who loves Christ desires to be an active member of a church. The person also practices sexual purity in the rela-tionship. The person produces the fruit of the Spirit: love, joy, peace, patience, kindness, faithfulness, gentleness, and self-control. The person serves you, listens to you, and treats you with respect.

Does this describe the person you are dating? Does this list describe you? As you read and study the Bible, be sure you are taking action on what you are reading. If you don't take action and do what the Word says, then you may become just like Mike, the wanna-be scuba man. Follow through on what God is telling you to do today, and by His Spirit, you will become more like Christ.

FURTHER SCRIPTURAL MEDITATION
- James 2:14–25
- Matthew 7:21–26
- Luke 6:46–49

Summarize, in your own words, the essence of this day's devotional on God's Word. Write down any thoughts, feelings, or insights in the space below.

Heavenly Father, forgive me for mistaking knowledge of Your Word for obedience to Your Word. Empower me today to be a true follower of Christ and live out the clear instructions You have given us in Your Word. Amen.

Dear God,

You are strong and mighty. You are holy and pure. There are no other gods above You. Lord, You know when I sit down and when I rise. You know every word I will speak before I even utter a sound. You have planned every day of my life before I was born. You are everywhere present.

God, You are so gracious to give us the Bible, which is the only true story of who You are and how You have provided a way for us to know You through Your Son, Jesus Christ. Thank You for the promises and power I receive when I study and apply Your Word to my life. Teach me on a daily basis what the Bible is saying and how to make that a reality in my job and relationships. Help me to hide Your truth in my heart and strengthen me during times of temptation.

Give me the diligence to read Your Word consistently, and may I seek to discover Your will for my life as I turn the pages. I affirm that Your Word is true, right, and pure. May my mind be transformed by the power of the Spirit as I soak in the Scriptures. I pray that I will learn to feed on the promises found in the Bible, so Your words will truly be my bread.

In the name of Jesus. Amen.

Prayer Journal

PRAISE (ADORATION):

REPENTANCE (CONFESSION):

APPRECIATION (THANKSGIVING):

YIELD (REQUESTS):

A Foundation of the Word

*T*oday we invite you and your partner to find a relaxing and peaceful setting to discuss the topic of *the Word*. The purpose is to ask questions, listen with compassion, and share with each other about your experiences regarding the issue for this past week. Remember, this is not a time to debate or argue about theological perspectives. This is a time to listen and seek to understand each other with a spirit of support and encouragement. Ultimately this venture together is intended to build a stronger foundation of spiritual intimacy.

This week we have explored the various reasons why you need to fill your heart and mind with God's Word. We have challenged you to consider the value of God's teaching to help you navigate upstream against the current of the world's system. You have also come to appreciate the importance of healthy, godly self-talk. Filling your mind with Scripture and God's truth has a significant impact on your physical, emotional, and spiritual well-being. Most important, you understand that God's primary vehicle for leading and guiding you is His Word.

QUESTIONS FOR DISCUSSION

1. Do you have a regular time and place for meditating on God's Word?

2. How can you inspire each other to maintain regular study of Scripture?

3. What is your greatest barrier to studying God's Word?

4. Discuss with each other your particular approach to "renewing your mind" with the Word.

5. Talk with your partner about the difficulties you've experienced in discovering the will of God. How does your view of Scripture help you discern God's will?

6. What else can you share with your partner concerning this topic?

SUNDAY

SERMON NOTES:

INSIGHTS TO SHARE:

WEEK FIVE

Simplicity

Simplicity is the ultimate sophistication.

—LEONARDO DA VINCI

Life is a succession of moments.
To live each one is to succeed.

—CORITA KENT

Simplicity is freedom.

—RICHARD FOSTER

Less is more.

—ANONYMOUS

Faster, Faster, Faster

Do not store up for yourselves treasures on earth . . . For where your treasure is, there your heart will be also.

—MATTHEW 6:19, 21

Frank was born into a family of immense wealth and prosperity. He had access to all kinds of worldly pleasures. He knew prominent people, and he enjoyed extravagant luxuries. One day, while sitting in church at the age of twenty-seven, he heard God's voice calling him to the ministry. Right in the middle of church, he stood up, stripped down, handed his expensive clothes to his father, and walked out of church bare naked to embrace a life of poverty, chastity, and asceticism. You probably know Frank by his other name, Saint Francis of Assisi, the beloved saint of the Middle Ages. Well, that's certainly one way to achieve a life of simplicity, and it may sound appealing in this fast-paced, consumeristic culture in which we live, but please don't try it at your home church. There's a better way.

I think it could be argued that never before in the history of mankind has there been a greater need for simplicity. A recent survey indicates that most American adults are increasingly looking for a way to simplify their lives. We are anxious, overwhelmed, overworked, and we can't seem to say no! Not only are we living life in the fast lane, but we seem to be accelerating the pace. In his book *Faster*, James Gleick says, "If one quality defines our modern technocratic age, it is acceleration. We are making haste. Our computers, our movies, our sex lives, our prayers—they all run faster now than ever before. And the more we fill our lives with time saving devices and time saving strategies, the more rushed we feel."

Isn't that ironic! We've become a quick-reflexed, multitasking, channel-flipping, fast-forwarding, instant-gratification species. More clothes, more money, more things, more trips, more projects, more, more, more. And we've got to have it faster, faster, faster. I think it's fair to conclude that we are slaves to many of our modern high-tech gadgets and "luxuries." As Richard Foster writes in his book *The Celebration of Discipline*, "Simplicity is freedom. Duplicity is bondage. Simplicity brings joy and balance. Duplicity brings anxiety and fear." So what about you? Are you experiencing personal freedom, inner joy, and a balanced life, or do you long for simplicity?

Achieving a life of simplicity must begin on the inside. It starts with the heart and eventually leads to an outward manifestation. We often get it backward by attempting to start on the outside and moving inward. Sometimes we can start by giving up certain behaviors and responsibilities, but ultimately it's an illusion to think we can surrender possessions, wealth, or even a busy schedule without also having an inner change.

All true simplicity begins by having a single purpose in life. You must decide to live your life based upon a unified purpose.

The book of Romans provides a clue to the grand purpose of life. You are called to be in the world but not of it. When you stray from God, you get caught up in the world's system and lose sight of your main purpose.

Your priorities should be different. Your perspectives should be eternal, and the way you define success should be based upon God's standards. Subsequently your main purpose as a Christian is *to glorify God in everything!* You live for Him, you worship Him, and you seek to obey Him in all that you do. Your single purpose is wrapped around God. He is the starting point for attaining a life of simplicity.

FURTHER SCRIPTURAL MEDITATION
- Ecclesiastes 3:12–13
- Philippians 4:6–8
- Hebrews 13:5

Summarize, in your own words, the essence of this day's devotional on the simple life. Write down any thoughts, feelings, or insights in the space below.

Dear God, help me to appreciate my need for simplicity. Give me the courage to make lifestyle and attitude changes in order to bring about greater simplicity in my life. Amen.

Hold On Loosely

Seek ye first the kingdom of God, and his righteousness; and all these things shall be added unto you.

—MATTHEW 6:33 KJV

Don't you just hate it when you lose your keys? Just as I (Sam) was walking out the door the other day, I realized I didn't have them. I was going to be late to an important meeting. I had things to do and people to see. But I couldn't even leave my house without my keys: keys to my car, keys to my office, keys to my files. I was paralyzed and helpless without them. All of a sudden my fast-paced world came to a screeching halt. I had to immediately realign my priorities, and I was consumed with my one new passion—I had to find my keys. It seems a simple task—to find my otherwise insignificant and unappreciated keys—but it became an essential and mandatory part of my day.

God's role in our lives is much like that of our keys—often overlooked, unappreciated, and definitely taken for granted. Yet His presence in our lives is so fundamental that without Him we might as well shut down our busy schedules. Jesus reminded us that in the midst of everything going on in our lives, we are to seek Him first (Matt. 6:33).

The Greek word for *seek* literally translated means "to be in a continual process of striving for and/or searching after." In other words, we should continually strive for God's agenda and His priorities. For a long time I misinterpreted this verse to suggest that I could do something "spiritual" for God first (maybe an early morning devotional), then carry out the rest of the day for myself, according to my agenda. What a misconception! I missed the whole point.

The most effective way to keep this priority in place is to surrender yourself—your life, your work, your all—into God's hands on a daily basis. Not surprisingly you must hold your own agenda very loosely. In effect, you wake up every single morning with the *attitude* that says, "God, I am willing to let go of my wishes, my desires, my goals, my dreams, my pride, my reputation, and my will if they don't fall in line with Yours. Lord, I accept Your wishes, Your desires, Your goals, and Your dreams for me this day."

Of course, many times your goals and desires coincide with God's. He puts them there! You can best accomplish this attitude of surrender by having a strong conviction that God is at work in your life and that He has grand purposes for you. Recognize that God is sovereign and ultimately in control of all things. Have the confidence that God is even involved in the situations that seem to be difficult or negative; that everything has been "ordained" by God. Believe that He has allowed everything to go through His hands first before it ever gets to you. He is intimately involved with you and aware of every detail of your life, working everything out according to His purpose. Romans 8:28 assures us, "We know that in all things God works for the good of those who love him, who have been called according to his purpose."

When you realign your priorities and you are willing to relinquish your agenda, you lose the preoccupation with the need for more status, power, and possessions. Slowly but surely you get rid of frivolous activities, nonessential tasks, and over-burdening responsibilities. You become clear and focused on what is necessary. Most important, you experience inner peace and freedom from worry. In other words, all the things you typically worry about will fall into place. Do you worry about money, food, clothing, financial or emotional security, fulfill-ment, reputation, or anything else for that matter? Do you long for simplicity? If you do, then seek first the kingdom of God, and all these things will be taken care of for you.

FURTHER SCRIPTURAL MEDITATION
- Isaiah 26:3
- Matthew 6:25–34
- Colossians 3:1–2

Summarize, in your own words, the essence of this day's devo-tional on the simple life. Write down any thoughts, feelings, or insights in the space below.

Lord, help me to seek You first in everything I do. Give me a godly perspec-tive and help me to realign my priorities in order to keep You first. Amen.

Just a Little Bit More!

No one can serve two masters. Either he will hate the one and love the other, or he will be devoted to the one and despise the other. You cannot serve both God and Money.

—MATTHEW 6:24

Someone once asked billionaire Nelson Rockefeller how much money it would take to satisfy a man. His answer: "Just a little bit more!" Can you identify with that struggle? We certainly do at times. It seems we are seldom satisfied with what we have. Perhaps one of the most powerful lies of Satan is the notion that something outside ourselves (money, possessions) can fill the thirst deep within. This idea keeps us on the never-ending quest for more, bigger, and better.

In reality only Christ can quench our thirst at the depth of our souls. Without Christ at the center of our lives, we will expend much of our emotional and physical energy buying things we don't necessarily need, with money we certainly don't have, in order to impress people that we don't even like.

Did you know the Bible has more to say about money and economic issues than just about any other subject? Jesus spent much of His three-year ministry speaking out against the materialism of that day. Isn't that intriguing, given the fact that He was speaking to members of a very simple agrarian society who were not necessarily affluent or materialistic compared to our standards? How much more do we need to heed the advice and counsel of Scripture concerning money and materialism? The not-so-subtle implication from Matthew 6:24 is that money can become your god. He is literally saying that money itself has the potential to serve as an idol. And Christ is asking you—and everyone else—to daily choose one or the other. You cannot have both.

So what is the key? It starts with a daily attitude of *thankfulness*. When Christ fills your soul and you readjust your focus on the things with which He has already blessed you, you have begun the process. Thank God for your salvation, for Christ who is in you and who can meet your every need. Thank Him for the gift of life, for your health, and for the senses of taste, touch, smell, sight, and hearing that allow you to experience the various aspects of life. Thank God for your gifts, talents, and skills by name. Thank Him for the beauty of nature, the sunrise you observe in the morning, the scenery you experience on the way to work. Thank Him for your friendships and the love you experience through each of these relationships.

Do you notice something curious about the items on this list? Can you appreciate the common denominator? Not one thing represents a material possession. The items do not cost a dime, and they are available to all. In effect, the things that are most valuable and bring the greatest pleasure and contentment are gifts from God.

FURTHER SCRIPTURAL MEDITATION

- Psalm 37:16
- Philippians 4:11–19
- 1 Timothy 6:6–11

Summarize, in your own words, the essence of this day's devotional on the simple life. Write down any thoughts, feelings, or insights in the space below.

Father, I confess my love of money and my obsession with materialism. Help me to realize that only You can satisfy the deep thirst in my soul. Amen.

Clock Ticking

The hour has come for you to wake up from your slumber, because our salvation is nearer now than when we first believed. The night is nearly over; the day is almost here. So let us put aside the deeds of darkness and . . . clothe yourselves with the Lord Jesus Christ.

—ROMANS 13:11–12, 14

*I*magine for a moment that your physician announced that you had only six months to live. Close your eyes for sixty seconds, put yourself in that position, and wait for the thoughts and feelings to arise. Among other things, I bet your perspectives changed and your values shifted. When we put ourselves in that position, all of a sudden, the things that matter most seem to bubble to the surface. What thoughts came up for you? Maybe you thought about your loved ones and your need to affirm your affection toward them. Perhaps you thought about investing in eternal things or the strength of your relationship with God. One way or another, the notion that your earthly life has a definite end gives you perspective and a sense of urgency about the things that matter most.

The late Francis Schaeffer once observed, "Life is like a clock that has no hands; you can hear the sound of the clock ticking but you don't know what hour it is." How true. Somewhere deep down in the recesses of your soul, you're aware that time is marching forward and death is imminent; you just don't know when. Paul told us in Romans 13 that we should live as though these are our last days. He said that we should not be so pre-occupied with our daily responsibilities that we lose sight of the bigger picture. Without eternal perspective, we live as though we are asleep. Paul urged us to wake up!

How can you establish this perspective when all you hear is the clock ticking? Two things are essential. First, remind your-self that today is the only day guaranteed to you. Yesterday is over. Tomorrow may never come. Robin Williams highlighted this point in the movie *The Dead Poets Society*. As a professor at a private school, he encouraged his students by saying, "Carpe diem (seize the day)!" He was right. We must intentionally set out to live in the present and to live this day to the fullest, keeping in mind that each day we are presented with a unique opportunity to make an eternal significance.

Second, clothe yourself with Christ. That was Paul's way of saying that you are to let Christ live His life through you. When you put on clothes, they become a part of you for that day. They reflect what you choose to present to the world. In the same way you are encouraged to put on Christ so that He may hang on you like clothes and you may present the quali-ties of Christ to the world around you.

In Galatians 3:27, Paul declared that we "who were baptized into Christ" have been clothed "with Christ." My seven-year-old son was baptized in front of the church in a large pool of water.

As the pastor lowered him beneath the surface of the water (we submerge the whole body from head to foot), he said, "Buried with Christ in death, raised to walk in a new kind of life." When my son came up from the water, he exclaimed, "Wow, that was fun! I want to do that every day!" In a sense, that is exactly what our reaction should be every morning of our lives. We metaphorically take the plunge; we bury ourselves in the water of redemption, and we emerge a new person, putting on Christ.

Need some perspective? Do you want to live today for the things that matter most? Take Paul's advice. Remind yourself that the Lord's coming is one day closer. Live life with a sense of urgency about the things that matter most. And put on Christ so that He may live His life through you. Seize the day!

FURTHER SCRIPTURAL MEDITATION
- Romans 13:11–14
- 2 Corinthians 5:17
- Ephesians 4:22–24

Summarize, in your own words, the essence of this day's devotional on the simple life. Write down any thoughts, feelings, or insights in the space below.

God, I admit that sometimes I act as though this life is never-ending. Help me to make the most of each day, and give me an eternal perspective. Amen.

Sitting at the Feet of the Master

Martha, Martha, . . . you are worried and upset about many things, but only one thing is needed. Mary has chosen what is better, and it will not be taken away from her.

—LUKE 10:41–42

"Hi, how are you?" "Oh, doing fine. Just real busy. Busy, busy, busy. You know, packed schedule, lots of meetings, people to see and places to go!" I'll bet you had that conversation with someone within the last twenty-four hours. Seems everyone is busy. Even the lazy guy with no job who sits around watching talk shows all day long will tell you that he's busy (watching television). Why? Because we live in a time and a culture that place a high premium on busyness. We applaud the workaholic. To be busy is to be valuable, successful, and important. Is that insane or what? What's worse is that our drive to stay busy keeps us distracted from the things that matter most.

The story of Martha and Mary in Luke 10 represents an excellent illustration of how to avoid the "busyness" trap. It's the story of Christ entering the home of two sisters, presumably for dinner. One of the sisters, Martha, was busy and distracted by all the preparations that had to be made in the kitchen. The other, Mary, was found sitting at the feet of Jesus, listening to what He was saying. Martha was busy doing things for Christ, while Mary took the time to humbly sit at His feet because she understood that she was in the presence of the Lord. This simple story is significant for those who desire a life of simplicity.

Because we live in an age of distraction, it's easy to fall prey to a form of spiritual mania—becoming hyperactive for God. Even the most well-meaning people can be distracted and preoccupied with "religion"—attending meetings, serving on committees, raising money for the cause of Christ, carrying out ministry projects. They are going through the motions of religiosity and doing things in the name of God and yet missing the higher call. Notice what Christ said to Martha in response to her complaint about her sister who was not helping her serve: "Martha, you are worried and bothered by so many things, but only a few things are necessary. Really, only one. Mary has chosen the good part, which shall not be taken away from her."

Jesus made it clear that the most essential thing you can do is to learn to sit at His feet and listen to His words. God doesn't necessarily need you to do anything for Him. He doesn't need your time, service, money, or talents to accomplish His will. He wants your heart and your devotion first. Then you are free to join Him in the things He is already doing. If you are overextended, rushing around, and even busy "doing" things for God, then don't just try to find a way to slow down. Rather, stop and sit down at the feet of the Master. You will have chosen "what is better."

FURTHER SCRIPTURAL MEDITATION

- Matthew 11:28–30
- Luke 10:38–42
- Philippians 3:7–9

Summarize, in your own words, the essence of this day's devotional on the simple life. Write down any thoughts, feelings, or insights in the space below.

Dear Father, may I learn to stop from time to time and just listen to Your voice. Help me to know the pleasure of sitting at Your feet. Amen.

Dear God,

Thank You that You are always here for me even when I have gotten busy with so many things and have forgotten to keep You first in my life. I praise You that You are the God of all and are sovereign over all the things that preoccupy me or cause me to worry.

I confess that I get busy doing too many things and put other things above my relationship and time with You. Help me to realign my priorities to seek You first and to live my life in light of Your kingdom purposes and values rather than those of the world. Lord, help me to see when I am living with wrong priorities. Please show me what things, activities, and people to remove from my life and where to spend my time and efforts.

Thank You for all the blessings in my life: my family, my friends, my church family, and most of all, my relationship with You through Jesus Christ. I thank You that You continue to hear my prayers and to help me grow to become more and more like the disciple of Christ that I wish to be.

In Jesus' name I pray. Amen.

Prayer Journal

PRAISE (ADORATION):

REPENTANCE (CONFESSION):

APPRECIATION (THANKSGIVING):

YIELD (REQUESTS):

A Foundation of Simplicity

*T*oday we invite you and your partner to set aside some time just for the two of you. We especially encourage you to find a relaxing and peaceful setting to discuss the topic of *simplicity*. Keep in mind that the purpose is to ask questions, listen with compassion, and share with each other about your experiences regarding the issue for this past week. This is a time to listen and seek to understand each other with a spirit of support and encouragement. Ultimately this venture together is intended to build a stronger foundation of spiritual intimacy.

This past week we have considered the importance of living a life of simplicity and how this discipline must start as an inward reality. You have learned that simplicity includes living with a unified purpose, an eternal perspective, and a sense of urgency about the things that matter most. You have also learned to slow down and consider how the pace of our society and the preoccupation with money affect you. And you have been encouraged to let Christ fill your deepest thirst for meaning and purpose as well as develop an attitude of thankfulness for the gifts that have been given to you by God. Discuss with your partner your answers to the following questions.

QUESTIONS FOR DISCUSSION

1. Do you long for a life of simplicity?

2. What's your version or interpretation of Matthew 6:33 ("Seek ye first the kingdom of God . . ." [KJV])?

3. How can you encourage each other in your priorities and perspectives?

4. What can you do, practically speaking, to simplify your life or your relationship?

5. Would you consider going on a personal weekend retreat to reestablish your priorities and perspectives?

6. Talk about your struggles with money, materialism, greed, and lust for more. Is there anything that you seem to idolize?

7. How can you inspire each other toward a life with greater simplicity?

8. How would you want to simplify your relationship?

9. What would you suggest in order to accomplish a greater degree of simplicity?

10. How could the discipline of simplicity in your life enhance your relationship together?

SUNDAY

SERMON NOTES:

INSIGHTS TO SHARE:

Forgiveness

To err is human, to forgive divine.

—ALEXANDER POPE

Forgiveness saves us the expense of anger,
the high cost of hatred, and the waste of energy.

—ANONYMOUS

Forgiveness is the most tender part of love.

—JOHN SHEFFIELD

Forgiveness is God's command.

—MARTIN LUTHER

Radical Forgiveness

If you forgive men when they sin against you, your heavenly Father will also forgive you.

—MATTHEW 6:14

Jesus Christ was a radical. He spoke radical words and did radical things. One of the most challenging concepts Christ talked about was forgiveness. Jesus said you must forgive others for the horrible things they have done to you. Okay, but He went on to say that if you do not forgive others when they hurt you, then your heavenly Father will not forgive you. That is radical!

For years we have tried to water down or soften the true meaning of this verse by looking at the original Greek or by consulting a commentary, but we simply cannot get around these hard-hitting words. How can you forgive those who have walked all over you or trampled on your heart? The key to extend radical forgiveness is to first realize that you are radically forgiven. Unforgiving people are unforgiven people; therefore, unless you have appropriated the forgiveness God offers you, you cannot forgive others.

Fortunately Jesus didn't just say radical words; He actually lived them out. When you walk through the pages of the Bible, you see a vivid picture of Jesus Christ forgiving people of their sins. In John 4, He met a woman at a local watering hole and told her where to find living water. The woman had been married five times and was currently living with another man. Christ extended forgiveness and life to this woman who was desperately in need of true love, and her whole life was transformed by her encounter with Christ. Radical forgiveness.

You probably remember the story of the woman caught in the act of adultery. She was thrown before religious leaders, who threatened to stone her to death for the immoral act. They said, "Jesus, the law says we must kill her! What do You say?" Christ said, "Those of you who have never lusted, you throw the first stone at this woman." Slowly the self-righteous men dropped their stones and walked away, until only Jesus and the woman caught in adultery remained. She was shaking with fear, curled up in the fetal position, anticipating the first strike from one of her "judges," when Jesus asked, "Woman, where are your accusers? Where are the people who seek to condemn you?" At that point we can imagine she was looking into the eyes of Jesus Christ, the Son of God, the only person who could really condemn her. He said, "They are all gone. They do not condemn you and neither do I. Go and sin no more." (See John 8.) Radical forgiveness.

Peter said that he would never deny Christ. Peter was known as the Rock, the superstar disciple who walked on water and proclaimed the true identity of Jesus while the others were still puzzled. He vehemently proclaimed that others might wimp out, but that he would never deny his Lord. We all know what happened. When Christ was taken away by the authorities and put on trial, Peter denied Jesus not once, not twice, but three times. When Jesus needed Peter the most, he disowned his Master like a big yellow coward. Can you imagine the guilt and shame that Peter must have carried? He had forsaken the Son of God during crunch time. He choked when it mattered the most. But the good news is that after His resurrection, Jesus forgave Peter completely, and Peter went on to become a key leader in the church. Radical forgiveness.

Today Jesus Christ extends His forgiveness to you. He does not excuse your sin, but through His sacrificial death on the cross, He forgives you and cleanses you of all your sins. You may be a good sinner, but Christ is a great forgiver! Put yourself in the sandals of the men and women of the Bible who experienced such forgiveness. You cannot invent a sin that can overpower the blood of Jesus Christ. Come clean with God today. Allow His forgiveness to invade your life so that you, too, may become a radical forgiver.

FURTHER SCRIPTURAL MEDITATION
- Matthew 18:21–35
- Mark 11:24–26
- Jeremiah 31:34

Summarize, in your own words, the essence of this day's devotional on forgiveness. Write down any thoughts, feelings, or insights in the space below.

Dear Lord, help me to understand the great depths of my sin and to receive the even greater reach of Your forgiveness to me. May I be ever mindful of both these truths so that I may be able to forgive those who have sinned against me. Amen.

Forgiveness Is Freedom

Forgive as the Lord forgave you.

—COLOSSIANS 3:13

*I*magine you are face-to-face with your father's murderer. This happened to a dear friend of mine (Sam) not too long ago. He took the opportunity to go into the jail and spend time with the very man who was convicted of killing his father—a senseless act of brutality. What would you have said to this man? Would you have given him a piece of your mind? Let him have it? That's not what my friend did. Through the power of the Holy Spirit, he actually found the courage to forgive this man and even lead him to salvation through Christ.

I'm not sure that I would have had the guts to do something that bold. Oh, sure, my friend had a "legitimate right" to hate this man and even seek revenge, but he understood that healing comes only through forgiveness. This true story illustrates the amazing power of forgiveness and highlights the fact that forgiveness is the only true option, no matter what the offense.

Often as a way to seek revenge, we fall into the trap of holding grudges or expecting something from those who hurt us. We assume that our anger and vengeful stance are legitimate ways of getting even, like holding someone hostage. The only problem is, when we harbor anger, resentment, bitterness, or hatred, we become the hostages.

A spirit of unforgiveness puts you in bondage and will affect you physically, emotionally, and spiritually. Many people report getting physically sick from internalized hatred and bitterness. Some doctors have even suggested a link between serious medical conditions such as cancer and unresolved, long-standing anger.

Refusal to forgive can also affect your emotional well-being. Becoming consumed with thoughts of revenge or being preoccupied with a need to punish the offender can affect your attitude and lead to emotional distress.

Some people expend a significant amount of time and mental energy obsessed with blame and hatred toward their offenders. In *The Art of Forgiving*, Lewis Smedes writes, "When we forgive someone we change the course of a meandering river that could, if we let it, carry us on an aimless, endless current of remembered hurt and frustrated rage."

Of course, unforgiveness will also affect your relationship with God. Deep down, you know that you have been forgiven by God and that you're capable of offenses similar to the one you won't forgive. Refusal to let go and forgive can lead to feelings of guilt and a damaged relationship with God. Are you prone to hold grudges and slow to release hurts? Are you imprisoned by your hatred? Do you tend to harbor a spirit of unforgiveness? Don't let yourself believe the lie that says, "It is better to get even." Instead, tap into the power to heal the wounds of your past and choose the way of forgiveness. Remember, forgiveness is freedom.

FURTHER SCRIPTURAL MEDITATION

- Hebrews 8:11–13
- 1 John 1:8–10
- Isaiah 1:18
- Luke 23:34

Summarize, in your own words, the essence of this day's devotional on forgiveness. Write down any thoughts, feelings, or insights in the space below.

Father, bring to my mind those I have held in contempt and refused to forgive. Help me to release my offenders and keep me from the bondage of unresolved anger and bitterness. Teach me to forgive, just as You have forgiven me. Amen.

Forgiveness Is Not...

"In your anger do not sin": Do not let the sun go down while you are still angry.

—EPHESIANS 4:26

*E*ric made an inner vow that he would never forgive his former best friend, Kenny. Kenny had betrayed Eric's trust and deeply wounded him forever. Eric feared that offering forgiveness would somehow minimize the offense and let Kenny off the hook. There are so many people in the world just like Eric. They walk around holding grudges, refusing to forgive someone who has wronged them because they do not fully understand the truth about forgiveness. Let's look at some classic misconceptions that keep people stuck in a cycle of hurt and anger.

Have you ever heard anyone say, "Well, you haven't truly forgiven someone unless you have forgotten; you must forgive and forget"? Most of the time, it is impossible to forget about hurts and wounds from the past. Forgetting is a form of brain damage! Only God has the power to "forget" our offenses. In the book of Psalms, we learn that God removes our transgressions (from His mind) as far as the east is from the west. But we do not have that supernatural capacity to forget, nor should we want to. In fact, we believe that remembering the offense is actually a step toward healing.

Being forgiving is not excusing, minimizing, or tolerating the offense. Some people fear that forgiveness is a form of putting up with an offense or communicating that what happened is really no big deal. That was Eric's problem. He felt that if he forgave Kenny, he would be sweeping the event under the rug, minimizing the pain he inflicted. The Bible instructs us to be angry and yet not sin. It's okay, even legitimate, to feel angry when we are wronged.

When you give yourself permission to fully acknowledge the hurt and its ramifications, in a sense to "be angry and sin not," you confront the truth about what happened. And by the way, you are not required to expose yourself to more hurt after you have forgiven the offender.

Forgiveness is not necessarily about reconciling with the offender. We have met scores of people who believe that if you truly forgive someone, you are obligated to reunite with that person. Let's remember that forgiveness is primarily for you and something that you do inside yourself. It takes only one person to forgive; it takes two to reconcile. In some situations, reconciliation is not desirable or even possible.

We encourage you to search your assumptions about the nature of forgiveness. Seek to clarify any faulty beliefs you may have and pray that God will inspire you to have a new perspective and appreciation for the value of forgiveness. Don't let another day pass without considering your need to forgive others.

FURTHER SCRIPTURAL MEDITATION
- Psalm 79:8–10
- Luke 17:1–4
- Psalm 103:11–12

Summarize, in your own words, the essence of this day's devotional on forgiveness. Write down any thoughts, feelings, or insights in the space below.

God, help me to appreciate the value and true meaning of forgiveness. Thank You that we can release our offenses and hurts to You. Amen.

How to Forgive

Be kind to one another, tenderhearted, forgiving one another, even as God in Christ forgave you.

—EPHESIANS 4:32 NKJV

$\mathcal{D}$orie Van Stone knows the healing power of forgiveness. As a child she was abandoned by her father and beaten by her mother. She eventually wound up in four different foster homes where she continued to be beaten and was also sexually molested. Some people who undergo such severe trauma may spend a lifetime angry, alone, and fearful, trying to make sense out of such injustice. That was not the case with Dorie. When she was a teenager, someone shared with her about the love of Jesus Christ and the forgiveness He offers to anyone who will turn from sins and trust in Him. She received Christ and later married a godly man. Today, she travels the world teaching others about the healing power of God's grace and the necessity to forgive those who have hurt them.

She writes in her book, *No Place to Cry*, "We can choose to forgive whether we feel like it or not. Forgiveness is not an emotion but an act of the will." If you are waiting until you *feel* like forgiving someone, you may never forgive him. Forgiveness flows from a decision, an act of your will. Even though every fiber in your body cries out in protest—"Don't do it; retaliate; hold on to the grudge no matter what"—you must tell the voices to be quiet in the name of Jesus. Forgiving someone is an event followed by a process, but it starts when you make the faith–filled decision of your will to forgive.

The next step in the process of forgiveness is to honestly come to terms with the offense. We refer to this as "assessing the damages." In other words, true forgiveness requires a full acknowledgment of the pain, hurt, and loss associated with the offense. Forgiveness is not about sweeping the offense under the carpet and saying, "Oh, that was no big deal." You must acknowledge the pain and allow yourself to access the feelings before you can forgive.

The final step in the process of forgiveness is to release the offender into the hands of God. Realize that God is a righteous Judge, and He will take care of any retaliation that is necessary (Rom. 12:19). You do not have to worry about whether God will let this person get away with it. Either he will experience the grace of God in his own life, or God will fully punish him on the day of final judgment. It is not your place to sit in judgment over anyone. God will take care of His children and those who have harmed them.

It goes without saying that you and I don't really have the power to forgive others in our human strength. Therefore, the entire process of forgiveness requires that you turn to God for supernatural strength. Meditate on how He has forgiven you; remember the debt from which He has released you. Christ died on the cross so that you might be cleansed of your filth and totally forgiven of all the times you have broken God's law. When Christ was dying on the cross, He looked down and forgave the soldiers who were executing Him. Ask God to give you that kind of supernatural strength to forgive those who have hurt you.

As you have explored the virtue of forgiveness over this past week, more than likely God has brought someone to your attention for you to forgive. If that is the case, then let us encourage you to do just that and make the decision to forgive the person. Acknowledge to God or a trusted friend the pain and hurt that you have experienced. Pray that He would give you the strength and courage to extend forgiveness. Release the offender into the hands of the righteous Judge who will do what is right.

FURTHER SCRIPTURAL MEDITATION

- Psalm 32:1–2
- Romans 12:9
- Hebrews 8:11–13

Summarize, in your own words, the essence of this day's devotional on forgiveness. Write down any thoughts, feelings, or insights in the space below.

Father, give me the courage to forgive those responsible for my deepest offenses. Help me to trust You more as the righteous Judge and to release them to You as I forgive. Amen.

Forgiveness in Marriage

Be compassionate, just as your Father is compassionate.

—LUKE 6:36 NLT

*M*ost of us are familiar with the story of the prodigal son. On the surface it is about the rebellious son who left home, foolishly squandered his share of the inheritance, and then came "crawling" back to his daddy, expecting anything but forgiveness or love. However, instead of being shamed, punished, or rejected, the son was received by his father with open arms, unconditional love and acceptance, and most of all, forgiveness. The father wasn't concerned with where the boy had been. He didn't even wait for repentance or remorse; the father had already forgiven him. He was concerned only with the restored relationship. The father was consumed with joy because his son who was once lost had returned. This is one of the greatest stories Jesus ever told to illustrate the love and forgiveness of our heavenly Father.

Have you ever wondered about the rest of the story? What happened years later to the prodigal son? Did he take advantage of his father's love? Did he go off and repeat his foolishness? We think not. In fact, there is no doubt that the impact of his reunion with the father changed his heart forever. The son was so blown away by his father's compassion that he went on to become just like his father—loving, compassionate, and forgiving. As Henri Nouwen has observed in his book *The Prodigal,* "A child does not remain a child. A child becomes an adult. When the prodigal son returns home, he returns not to remain a child but to claim his sonship and become a father himself."

God is calling each of us, as His child who has returned home, to move beyond the position of son or daughter and begin to exhibit that kind of compassion and forgiveness in all relationships. This applies most particularly in the marriage relationship. After all, what is marriage but a decision to unite two hearts and build one home together? The marriage relationship should be a place where we are continuously received with open arms—the one place where we can be safe, secure, and accepted unconditionally. When you make a decision to unite with a partner in marriage, in effect you are saying, "I am committed to providing for you a safe haven—a place of acceptance, compassion, and forgiveness."

I would venture to say that one of the most essential resources for a successful marriage is the tool of forgiveness. Here's why. Marriage at times can bring out your best, but it will certainly bring out your worst. The marriage relationship will eventually expose your faults, selfishness, and imperfections. It is within this context that you will experience your greatest joys but also your greatest disappointments. Therefore, any successful relationship between two imperfect, flawed individuals must be bathed in an atmosphere of mutual forgiveness.

How would you evaluate your ability to forgive others? Do you demonstrate an open-arms approach with your partner? Ask God to help you learn the art of forgiveness. Learn to be compassionate as your Father in heaven is compassionate.

FURTHER SCRIPTURAL MEDITATION
- Luke 15:11–32
- Ephesians 5:25–33
- Luke 7:40–43
- Hosea 2:19–20

Summarize, in your own words, the essence of this day's devotional on forgiveness. Write down any thoughts, feelings, or insights in the space below.

Dear Father, help me to live with an attitude of compassion and forgiveness. Teach me to be the kind of person who can extend open arms with grace and mercy. May I continually grow in my ability to forgive as I mature in following Christ. Amen.

Prayer

Dear Lord,

Thank You for another day of life. Every breath I take is a gift from You. I praise You because You are all-knowing and all-powerful. You know my past, present, and future; there are no surprises to You. God, You are the only One who can forgive me of all the many times I have failed You and broken Your commandments. Thank You for sending Jesus Christ to die in my place so that I might be fully forgiven by His blood. Help me to appropriate and receive this incredible forgiveness in my life, no matter what my emotions say.

Father, because You have forgiven me of such an incredible debt, empower me to forgive those who have hurt me. There is no way that I can forgive others without Your strength. Help me to make a decision of my will to release these persons of the debts they owe me. Yes, I know it was hurtful and painful, but I do not want this poison of unforgiveness flowing through my body. I release them into Your hands as the righteous Judge of the universe. You alone are God.

In Jesus' name I pray. Amen.

Prayer Journal

PRAISE (ADORATION):

REPENTANCE (CONFESSION):

APPRECIATION (THANKSGIVING):

YIELD (REQUESTS):

A Foundation of Forgiveness

*T*oday we challenge you and your partner to set aside some time for the two of you. We encourage you to find a peaceful setting to discuss the topic of *forgiveness.* Keep in mind that the purpose is to ask questions, listen with compassion, and share with each other about your experiences regarding the issue for this past week. This is not a time to debate or argue about theological perspectives. You are to listen and seek to understand each other with a spirit of support and encouragement. Ultimately this venture together is intended to build a stronger foundation of spiritual intimacy.

This week we have discussed the key to ongoing relational success—forgiveness. You have learned that forgiveness is really not an option for Christians; it is a commandment from God Himself that we forgive even as He forgave us. You've considered the fact that true forgiveness is an act of the will and should not be dictated by your feelings. You've also been encouraged to clarify some misconceptions around forgiveness. And you understand that forgiveness is freedom; it is the most powerful resource you have to heal the wounds of a past that you cannot change.

Questions for Discussion

1. What have you found to be most helpful about this week's devotional regarding forgiveness?

2. How would you evaluate yourself in terms of having a spirit of forgiveness? Do you find that it comes naturally? Is it difficult?

3. Discuss with your partner the idea that *forgiveness is freedom.* Can you think of any examples from your past where this was true for you?

4. Do you need to forgive people in your life?

5. What about your dating partner? Are you holding on to any hurts or offenses that you need to acknowledge and let go of? Take some time now and clear the air between yourselves.

SUNDAY

SERMON NOTES:

INSIGHTS TO SHARE:

Community

Discovering the church is apt to be a slow procedure
but it can only take place if you have a free mind
and no vested interest in disbelief.

—FLANNERY O'CONNOR

The community of believers is the "context"
within which most of us will "recognize the Lord."

—DANIEL TAYLOR

No Lone Rangers

It is not good for the man to be alone.

—GENESIS 2:18

Since 1996, I (Ben) have hosted a live radio talk show for singles called *The Single Connection*. It has given me the opportunity to interact with thousands of singles from coast to coast on issues such as dating, sex, divorce, and single parenting. One of the first questions I typically ask people who call into the show is this: "Are you plugged into a local church in your city?" Too many times the response is "no" or "I hop around from church to church." It breaks my heart every time I hear this response because I know that God has created us to live in community with others, and when we neglect gathering with like-minded believers, we miss out on a multitude of blessings.

God designed you to connect with others in a meaningful way. He created you to be in close, intimate, and supportive relationships where you can experience trust, safety, and vulnerability. You are not an island or a Lone Ranger. You were made for community. The emptiness and longing that you feel in your heart today may be a direct result of your disconnection from fellow Christians.

The local church is God's new community on this planet. The church is not perfect because it is filled with imperfect people, but it is still God's means to reach a lost and hurting world. Christ laid down His life for the church. He is coming back for the church. When you trust Christ and enter a relationship with God, you are not making an isolated, individualistic decision. To come to Christ is also to join with the universal church here on earth.

Time and time again the New Testament refers to the church as the body of Christ. That means we are the physical manifestation of Jesus Christ on earth until He comes back. Just as the human body has various parts with various functions, the church operates in the same manner. If you were to lose your arm today, would you miss it? Of course you would. The church is missing a lot of body parts because of "Lone Ranger" Christians who want to do their own thing.

Not only does the church need you, but you need the church. You need people in your life who will encourage you and, when necessary, graciously confront you if you are headed down the wrong path. You need people who will listen to your deepest concerns and pray for you. You also need people who will love and comfort you when you are sick or hurting. You need a shoulder to lean on when you have lost someone you love. I don't know how certain people make it without the support and help of others.

If you are not currently involved in a local church, ask God to lead you to a healthy church in your area. If you are already a member of a church, then thank God for your spiritual family and make sure you are building relationships at your place of worship—not just warming a pew. Don't miss out on the rewards and benefits associated with being a part of God's kingdom here on earth!

FURTHER SCRIPTURAL MEDITATION
- Acts 2:44–47
- Galatians 6:9
- Hebrews 10:24–25

Summarize, in your own words, the essence of this day's devotional on community. Write down any thoughts, feelings, or insights in the space below.

Heavenly Father, thank You for the community of believers in my local church. Help me to be faithful in serving and relying on my church to live according to Your pattern of community for all believers. Amen.

What's in It for Me?

Consequently, you are no longer foreigners and aliens, but fellow citizens with God's people and members of God's household.
—EPHESIANS 2:19

We are a generation raised on Madison Avenue slogans: "You deserve a break today," "Have it your way," and L'Oréal assures you that "you're worth it." It's no wonder that the most fundamental question we ask about a new job, relationship, or business deal is, "What's in it for *me?*" Since the world seems to revolve around us, we demand to know from the start how this person, product, or new venture is going to benefit us. When we join a church, we often ask the same question.

Well, there are many benefits to being a member of a local church, but one of the most significant benefits is that you gain a new family. Most of us have some form of dysfunction from our homes or other past relationships. I (Ben) have rarely seen a home without its share of pain and dysfunction. Some of us have even been affected by the trauma of divorce. The emotional, psychological, and spiritual consequences of ruptured relationships, whether from home or other situations, are devastating. That's why I believe that the greatest benefit of being a Christian is that you are adopted into God's family. You receive the blessing of new spiritual parents and mentors who can teach you how to grow in your faith relationship with Christ.

For example, a close friend of mine comes from a rough family background marked by instability and rejection. When I pray with him now, one of the first things he thanks God for is that he has a new family—new brothers and sisters, new friends who will love, encourage, and support him. God often uses people in the church to re-parent those who need to see what it is like to be a godly husband and father or a godly wife and mother.

You and your partner may need to see what a healthy relationship looks like. At the very least you may avail yourselves of a mentoring relationship with an older, married couple who will support you and advise you along the path of engagement toward marriage. Young woman, you may need a "spiritual mom" who has traveled a little farther down life's path than you. Young man, you may need an example to show you what it means to be a spiritual leader and a man of integrity. Don't miss out on this incredible benefit.

If you find yourself asking, "What's in it for me?" then here it is: an entire set of relatives who will love you, pray for you, listen to you, and model for you what it means to follow Christ in relationships. By the way, don't be dismayed when you discover that some of your new brothers and sisters in the family of God are imperfect. Remember what Saint Augustine said: "We are all sin sick sinners looking for healing." Don't wait until you find the perfect church because it doesn't exist. It's common for people to rationalize, "Well, there are so many hypocrites in the church. That's why I don't join one." I agree that the church is not immune from having hypocrites among its members, but there are hypocrites everywhere. Just because I read an article in the newspaper about corruption in the fire department on Friday does not mean that I will fail to call the fire department on Saturday if my house catches fire.

Find a Bible-believing church in your area where you can connect relationally and spiritually and join that church. Don't miss out on this irreplaceable benefit of being a part of God's family.

FURTHER SCRIPTURAL MEDITATION

- Ecclesiastes 4:9–12
- Acts 4:32–33
- Ephesians 2:19–21

Summarize, in your own words, the essence of this day's devotional on community. Write down any thoughts, feelings, or insights in the space below.

God, lead me to a local church. I realize You created us to live and grow among Your family of believers; I want to live according to Your design for my life, and I need Your guidance in doing this. Amen.

One Another

*A new commandment I give to you, that you love one another, even as
I have loved you, that you also love one another. By this all men will
know that you are My disciples, if you have love for one another.*

—JOHN 13:34–35 NASB

$\mathcal{S}$ociologist and preacher Tony Campolo wandered into a
diner at 3:30 in the morning in Honolulu. He was suffering
from a case of jet lag and simply wanted something to eat.
While he was there, a group of boisterous prostitutes came in
and sat down at a table nearby. One prostitute, named Agnes,
proclaimed to the group that tomorrow was her birthday. All
of her friends chided her and made fun of her because of her
abrupt announcement. Agnes said, "Hey, take it easy. I just
wanted you to know. I'm not expecting you to throw a party or
anything. I have never had a party in my life. Why would I
want one now?"

After the prostitutes left the diner, Campolo asked the
owner if the gals came in there every night. The man behind
the counter said, "Yup." Then Campolo got the wildest idea
to throw a surprise birthday party for Agnes. At 2:30 the next
morning, Tony and the owner decorated the place and baked

a special birthday cake for the streetwalker. When she waltzed through the door around 3:00 A.M., she was stunned. She was so moved by the gesture of love that she did not touch the cake but immediately took it home, only to return to the party later.

When she left, Campolo found himself surrounded by prostitutes. Taken aback by the awkward moment, he decided to pray. After the prayer the man behind the counter said, "Hey, you never told me you were a preacher! What kind of church do you belong to anyway?" And Tony answered, "The kind of church that throws birthday parties for prostitutes at three-thirty in the morning."

What a wonderful story. What a wonderful act of love. God has called you to demonstrate His love and mercy to others in a creative way. The New Testament is full of commandments to love one another, pray for one another, encourage one another, give to one another, confess your sins to one another, heal one another, and lay down your lives for one another. Remember, *love* is a verb. Love is an action. Love is something you do.

How can you show the love of God to a fellow church member or a total stranger today? Maybe it is just as simple as smiling at everyone you lock eyes with today. Or maybe you can give bottled water and some food to a street person whom you usually ignore. Perhaps you can use fewer words in your interaction with others and instead attempt to focus on being a good listener. Speak a genuine word of encouragement or thanks to a colleague at work. Buy the coffee for your friends and serve them.

See if you can be creative or even extravagant with your love for one another. Pray that God would give you divine appointments and opportunities to love others as you go throughout this day that He has made. Oh, one word of caution: be careful what you pray for. He may put an Agnes in your path when you least expect it.

FURTHER SCRIPTURAL MEDITATION
- 2 Corinthians 1:3–5
- 1 Peter 4:8–11
- 1 John 4:11–12

Summarize, in your own words, the essence of this day's devotional on community. Write down any thoughts, feelings, or insights in the space below.

Lord, help me to follow Your example of extravagant love to those in my church family and local community. Show me new ways to practically love others and to continually look for opportunities to extend Your grace each day. Amen.

Use Your Gifts

We have different gifts, according to the grace given us. If a man's gift is prophesying, let him use it in proportion to his faith. If it is serving, let him serve; if it is teaching, let him teach; if it is encouraging, let him encourage; if it is contributing to the needs of others, let him give generously; if it is leadership, let him govern diligently; if it is showing mercy, let him do it cheerfully.

—ROMANS 12:6–8

My (Ben's) family is crazy about basketball. My two brothers and I played in high school, and my oldest brother played college ball at Florida State. We spent our formative years shooting hoops in damp gymnasiums or in our backyard. Growing up in the basketball country of North and South Carolina, we played against some of the toughest competition in the nation. But one of my most cherished memories of the game involves the creative cheers from our opponents' fans and cheerleaders. Whenever you shot a free throw, the cheerleaders would chant, "U-G-L-Y, you ain't got no alibi. You're ugly, boy, you're ugly." Or if they really hated you, they would add, "Your mama says, 'You're ugly.'" Another cheer still rings in my mind today. It goes like this: "You got it. Now use it. You got it. Now use it." I love this cheer, which is simple, yet powerful.

The problem of too many Christians today is that they don't know what they have, much less how to use it. When you become a Christian, God gives you a spiritual gift or various gifts to use in order to serve others in the church. One reason that the church in America is so anemic is that people are not using their spiritual gifts within the local church.

Let's take a look at some of these gifts—serving, hospitality, teaching, leadership, giving, faith, encouragement, preaching, and mercy, to name a few. We are to use gifts not to call attention to ourselves, but to build up the body of Christ. There are a variety of gifts that help maintain balance and force us to depend on one another. What would happen if your foot said to your leg, "See you later. I'm tired of this stinky job. I want to be an eye"? Your body would cease to function properly because a foot doesn't have the capacity to see.

Although you may not have the gift of teaching, you may have the gift of serving. You may desire to teach and that's great, but if God wired you to serve in a support role, you will be miserable trying to do something you are not equipped to do. One way to discover your gifts is to consider what you are truly passionate about. Many times, the things that we are naturally drawn to or are enthusiastic about correspond with our spiritual gifts. Another way to discover your gifts is to volunteer for various assignments at your church. Tell your pastor you are willing to do anything the church needs so that you can find your niche in the ministry. Often, the people around you will affirm your gifts.

You will be amazed at what God will do in your life and the lives of others when you begin to use these gifts. Be encouraged! God promises that each of us has various gifts to be used for His glory. You've got it. Now use it!

FURTHER SCRIPTURAL MEDITATION
- Romans 12:4–13
- 1 Corinthians 12
- Ephesians 4:7–16

Summarize, in your own words, the essence of this day's devotional on community. Write down any thoughts, feelings, or insights in the space below.

Dear Father, I want to be used in the church to serve You by serving others. Give me the courage to try new ministries and to find ways to be used in my church. Amen.

Take Off the Mask

Confess your sins to one another, and pray for one another, so that you may be healed.

—JAMES 5:16 NASB

A few years ago I injured my shoulder playing tennis and volleyball. After weeks of pain I finally paid a visit to the doctor and had an MRI done on my shoulder. Getting an MRI is like being buried alive. The technician puts you on a conveyer belt and asks you to remain perfectly still for thirty minutes. Then he goes into the other room and pushes a button, and the belt pulls you into a narrow cylinder where the walls are about four inches from your face.

I was in the chamber about twenty seconds when I suddenly felt the urge to scream out, "Don't close the casket. I'm still alive!" Eventually a voice asked, "Are you okay in there?" And of course, I faked it and said, "Sure, I'm fine; I'm okay." Somehow by the grace of God I survived the frightening experience.

We live in an "I'm okay, you're okay" world. When we ask people how they are doing, we don't necessarily expect an honest answer. A simple "I'm fine" will suffice. Most of us fear letting others know what is rumbling deep inside our souls. We suspect that if people really knew what was going on with us on the inside, they might reject us. Too many of us walk around wearing masks, smiling on the outside but hurting on the inside. We are all afraid, but we act as if everything is fine, just as I did in that MRI tunnel.

The truth is, many times I'm not okay, you're not okay, but that's okay. Jesus died on the cross for folks like you and me, sinners who have broken God's laws time and time again. Remember what Saint Augustine said, "The church is a hospital, where everyone is trying to get well." However, you cannot get well unless you are willing to admit you are sick. The verse today on confession presupposes that we are all sick and in need of a doctor.

Confession has gotten a bad rap over the past thirty years. Television sitcoms, movies, and songs love to mock a guilt-ridden priest hearing the confession of a fellow guilt-ridden sinner. Yet Dietrich Bonhoeffer once wrote, "A man who confesses his sins in the presence of a brother knows that he is no longer alone with himself; he experiences the presence of God in the reality of the other person." In other words, when we confess to one another, forgiveness and healing become real to us. Whoever said confession is good for the soul was absolutely right!

Some of the greatest spiritual breakthroughs in my life have occurred when I took off my mask in the presence of a trusted friend and said, "Hey, I'm tired of hiding. I'm tired of living a double life. Here is what I am dealing with." And to have that friend listen to me and affirm that I am forgiven because of what Christ did for me on the cross is an extremely cathartic experience. As a pastor, I have had the incredible opportunity to see many people experience the freedom from guilt, shame, fear, and addiction because they had the courage to confess their sin.

If you are living in fear that someone is going to find out about the real you, do not hesitate to get help. Call a fellow member of your church, a pastor, or a counselor, and deal with that issue today. Ask God for the courage to take that first step.

FURTHER SCRIPTURAL MEDITATION
- Isaiah 1:18
- Galatians 6:1–2
- 1 John 1:7–9

Summarize, in your own words, the essence of this day's devotional on community. Write down any thoughts, feelings, or insights in the space below.

Dear God, give me the courage to practice confession with a trusted Christian in my church. Help me to confess regularly so that I may be free of the guilt and bondage of sins and free to grow together with my brothers and sisters in Christ. Amen.

Dear Father,

I praise You for Your justice and Your mercy. You are holy, and You are loving. Your physical and spiritual blessings are new every morning. You are faithful and kind when I have been faithless and cold.

Thank You for the replenishing power of relationships. Thank You for designing us to connect with others in a deep and meaningful way. I know You have created us to live in harmony and community with others. Forgive me, Father, for the many times I have tried to do my own thing and live a solo life. There is no way I can live this Christian life without the help and encouragement of others.

God, I ask that You would show me how I can get involved in my church. Help me to discover my spiritual gifts and to use them to build up others around me. Give me an attitude of one who seeks to serve rather than one who is always taking. Keep me forever connected with a local church wherever I go and whatever I do.

In Jesus' name. Amen.

Prayer Journal

PRAISE (ADORATION):

REPENTANCE (CONFESSION):

APPRECIATION (THANKSGIVING):

YIELD (REQUESTS):

A Foundation of Community

$\mathcal{T}$oday we want you and your partner to set aside some time to discuss the topic of *community*. Keep in mind that the purpose is to ask questions, listen with compassion, and share with each other about your experiences regarding the issue for this past week. This is not a time to debate or argue about theological perspectives. This is a time to listen and seek to understand each other with a spirit of support and encouragement. Ultimately this venture together is intended to build a stronger foundation of spiritual intimacy.

For the past week, we have addressed the importance of Christian community. We've looked at the idea that when any-one decides to trust Christ, he is making a decision to join the church, that is, the community of God's family. We've discussed the benefits of joining a local church for you and for the specific body of believers with which you become associated. You understand that the church is a place to let down your mask and be genuine. It's a place to develop intimate, supportive, and safe relationships to help you deal with life's many challenges.

QUESTIONS FOR DISCUSSION

1. Are you and your partner a member of a local church? If not, why not?

2. Discuss your past experiences with church.

3. Discuss your fantasy of the ideal church in order to clarify the things that you value most with the understanding that there is no "perfect" church this side of heaven.

4. Discuss what you believe to be the greatest benefits of being involved in a community of fellow believers.

5. Have you developed the close, intimate kinds of relationships that allow you to be encouraged, supported, and even challenged?

6. Do you know what your spiritual gifts are? Are you exercising these gifts?

7. Was there anything else from the lesson this past week that you have a strong reaction about? Feel free to discuss.

Sunday

(Today's Date)

Sermon Notes:

Insights to Share:

WEEK EIGHT

Purity

Sexual love has its source in God's own being, in His nature . . .
And so the sex act itself may be said to be in God's likeness,
fashioned in His own image.

—MIKE MASON

God will always give us the strength
we need to keep purity as
something beautiful for God.

—MOTHER TERESA

Blessed are the pure in heart, for they will see God.

—JESUS CHRIST

A Precious Gift

God created man in his own image, in the image of God he created him;
male and female he created them.

—GENESIS 1:27

I (Sam) was talking with a group of parents about our culture's obsession with sex and its effects upon our children. After listening to one parent rant and rave (for what seemed like eternity) about our society "idolizing sex," it suddenly dawned on me that we've got it backward. The initial assumption, of course, is that because of our cultural fixation on sexuality, we must have elevated it too high. The truth is that as a society, we have brought sex to a new low!

Although it's true that we have accentuated the sensual side of sex, we have somehow lost sight of its spiritual significance. When anyone assumes that sex is just a "physical thing," he cheapens sexuality and devalues this sacred act. We have reduced this glorious and sacred mystery to nothing more than a biological need, an erotic itch that must be scratched.

Consider what Mike Mason writes in his book *The Mystery of Marriage*: "Surely it was God's full intention for the physical joining together of a man and a woman to be one of the mountaintop experiences of life . . . in which He Himself might overshadow His people in love, might come down among them and be most intimately and powerfully revealed." You see, sexual love is not just a physical thing; it's a spiritual thing. And it's a glorious thing. That's why Paul exclaimed that it's a monstrosity for us to engage in sex outside marriage (1 Corinthians 6:15–17).

When did we actually begin to devalue sex (and sexuality) from the good that God intended it to be? Well, it didn't start with the sexual revolution of the sixties. It is common spiritual knowledge that everything about life and who we are as people has been tainted ever since the fall of Adam and Eve. The consequences of original sin reach into every corner of our lives, not the least of which is the sexual dimension. And one of the most tragic results of the Fall is the assumption that God wants nothing to do with sex. There is a distorted belief that sex is somehow unholy and unclean; that sexuality and spirituality are mutually exclusive. Nothing could be farther from the truth.

Sex starts with God. He is the Mastermind, the Creator of this beautiful experience, and He delights in our sexuality. So when it comes to purity, we must go back to the Garden and redefine sexuality. We must start at the beginning with a strong conviction that our sexuality is a gift from God. We must learn to appreciate and even celebrate this aspect of who we are.

Genesis 1:27 indicates that our distinct sexual differences as male and female somehow reflect the image of God. This represents, among other things, a statement about the goodness of our sexuality. In the New Testament, the apostle Paul said that everything created by God is good and nothing is to be rejected if it is received with thanksgiving (1 Timothy 4:4).

Genesis 2 goes on to affirm our sexuality: "The man and his wife were both naked, and they felt no shame" (v. 25). When we take this passage at face value (although there are also deeper implications), we must conclude that God intended for us to be unashamed about our masculinity and femininity. Far from being embarrassed or silent, we should be confident, even enthusiastic, about our sexuality. It's tragic that we may repress this valuable part of our makeup because of distortions and fears that are imposed upon us while growing up. In a way, an attempt to deny this significant part of our creation is insulting to God.

As with any gift that you value greatly, you would want to hold it up in high honor. A special gift is something you want to cherish and treat with care. Can you appreciate the notion that your sexuality is a gift from God? Are you willing to redefine sexuality as something sacred and holy? Believe it or not, the first step in maintaining sexual purity is embracing your sexuality because it is a precious gift from God.

FURTHER SCRIPTURAL MEDITATION

- Genesis 2:24–25
- 1 Corinthians 7:3–5
- James 1:17

Summarize, in your own words, the essence of this day's devotional on purity. Write down any thoughts, feelings, or insights in the space below.

Dear God, thank You for the wonderful gift of sexuality. Help me to cherish this part of Your creation and to respect it as something holy and sacred. Amen.

Sex and Wholeness

You will know the truth, and the truth will set you free.

—JOHN 8:32

*J*ust the other day, I dropped by the grocery store to pick up some milk, orange juice, and yogurt. As I stood in the so-called express lane, I read some of the covers on various magazines: "How to Turn Him On—Six Easy Steps"; "New Sex Positions Guaranteed to Work"; and "Sizzling Sex Tonight!" Can you believe it? You can't even buy a few simple items at the local grocery without being bombarded with overt sexual messages.

We live in a sexually saturated society. Mainstream America's party line on sex is simple: "If it feels good, do it." Mainstream Christianity's party line on sex is even simpler: "Don't do it." One side appears to have a positive slant on sex—"express yourself"—and the other side appears to have a negative slant on sex—"suppress yourself."

Growing up in the church, I always knew sex outside marriage was wrong, but I never really understood why. Sure, I knew all the sexual scare tactics on pregnancy, AIDS, and sexually transmitted diseases, but those reasons were negative. I began to wonder whether there were any positive, compelling reasons to save sex for marriage.

Yes, Virginia, there is a significant, positive reason to save sex for the confines of marriage, and here it is: *when you practice sexual purity in your relationship, saving sex until after the wedding, you will maintain your health and experience a sense of wholeness.* We've worked with thousands of men and women around the country who have experienced unbelievable emotional, physical, and psychological scarring because they believed the lie that sex brings you closer to your partner. If you just wear a condom, so the thinking goes, you can protect yourself from the nasty side effects of sex. Friends, you cannot put a condom around your soul; therefore, you are exposed and vulnerable to many levels of emotional hurt.

Saving sex for marriage keeps you from feeling scattered and helps protect you from shame, guilt, anxiety, and disintegration. The truth is, the more you continue to value your body and the significance of sexuality by waiting, the more secure, peaceful, and whole you will feel.

You can experience the hidden value of practicing sexual purity—personal peace, wholeness, and joy. Learn to celebrate and value the healthy choice you have made. Rick Stedman expresses it so well in his book *Your Single Treasure: The Good News About Singles and Sexuality:* "Sexual celibacy is the decision that sexuality is of value and personhood is special. When celibate, single adults are saying through their actions, 'I will not reduce my sexuality to a cheap giveaway. I will not pretend it is unimportant or insignificant. It is valuable, and I am valuable. I will assert my worth and value by saving myself until marriage.'"

Let this truth set you free today. Celebrate your self-worth and sense of wholeness. Thank God for the life-giving decision you and your partner have made to maintain purity. Saving sex for marriage is saying yes to wholeness and no to brokenness and insecurity. What an investment you can make with returns that correspond to God's ideal for you in marriage.

FURTHER SCRIPTURAL MEDITATION
- Genesis 2:23–24
- Psalm 119:1–2
- Song of Solomon 8:4

Summarize, in your own words, the essence of this day's devotional on purity. Write down any thoughts, feelings, or insights in the space below.

Father, I want Your ideal for marriage. Help me to appreciate the value of saving sex for marriage, and thank You for the peace that comes with maintaining purity. Amen.

Purity and Control

It is God's will that you should be sanctified: that you should avoid sexual immorality; that each of you should learn to control his own body in a way that is holy and honorable, not in passionate lust like the heathen, who do not know God; and that in this matter no one should wrong his brother or take advantage of him.

— 1 THESSALONIANS 4:3–6

*L*aura and Jimmy, childhood sweethearts who had never been apart for more than a week, found themselves ready for marriage at the ripe old age of twenty. Upon getting engaged and certain of their destiny, they decided to consummate their relationship as a way to celebrate their commitment to each other. They reasoned, "It's okay to begin a sexual relationship; we're already married in God's eyes anyway." But this couple never made it to the altar. Their fantasy of safety and commitment had no real basis; it was an illusion. Now they must face the ramifications.

Whenever we act on our sexual desires outside God's guidelines, we disregard the intended purpose of this sacred aspect of our lives. Sex outside marriage is not God's ideal for you because it takes something wonderful out of context. It's just like fire. When you light a fire in your fireplace, it can be a wonderful thing—it provides warmth, light, and energy in a contained space. However, when you take that same fire and place it outside its proper context (the middle of the living room floor), it blazes out of control and leads to untold damage and destruction.

In other words, when you divorce sexual love from the safe confines of marital commitment and responsibility, you (and your partner) will experience natural and spiritual consequences. Ultimately you cannot separate the sexual self from the emotional and spiritual self.

Sex is a life-uniting act, and it should be the result of intimacy and oneness within the context of a committed marriage. As harsh as this may sound, having sex outside marriage is usually about selfish exploitation. Sex then becomes a mutual agreement to use each other for mere pleasure. God makes it clear that you are to control your body in a way that is holy and honorable. Likewise, you should control yourself as a way to honor and respect your partner.

Therefore, you are encouraged to control your passions; to hold sexuality in high regard in order to protect yourself and others. Maintaining purity is not just about doing what is right, but it is about doing something that is good for you. Saving sex for marriage is a way to respect your worth and value. Saving sex for marriage is also about respecting your partner and giving him or her the dignity deserved.

Anyone who knows God in a personal way will strive to maintain purity both internally and externally. In other words, saving sex for its proper context will be one of his highest values. As a result a true Christ follower who falls in the sexual arena in thought or deed will always feel some sense of shame or guilt. He will be convicted by the Spirit and motivated to change. A true Christ follower appreciates the sacred component of sexuality. A true Christ follower honors the mystery of sex and seeks to save this life-uniting act for the safe and appropriate haven of marriage.

The counsel of Scripture regarding sex is a gracious attempt to save you from heartache and disillusionment. Let your desires and passions remind you of your need for emotional and spiritual intimacy. Rather than act on your impulses, channel your sexual energies into healthy endeavors and meaningful and supportive interaction with each other. Continue to build your foundation of closeness, safety, and trust so that you may experience God's best for your future.

FURTHER SCRIPTURAL MEDITATION
- Proverbs 7:4–5
- Isaiah 55:8–9
- Ephesians 5:3
- Song of Solomon 2:7

Summarize, in your own words, the essence of this day's devotional on purity. Write down any thoughts, feelings, or insights in the space below.

Lord, give me the strength and the motivation to set boundaries and maintain a sense of control in this most delicate arena. I commit to focus on other aspects of intimacy in order to save the physical for marriage. Amen.

We All Need a Little Help

*In the spring, at the time when kings go off to war . . . David remained
in Jerusalem. One evening David got up from his bed and walked
around on the roof of the palace. From the roof he saw a woman
bathing. The woman was very beautiful . . . Then David sent mes-
sengers to get her. She came to him, and he slept with her.*

—2 SAMUEL 11:1–4

From Jimmy Swaggart to Bill Clinton, Americans are accus-
tomed to sex scandals. There have been so many sexcapades
among preachers and politicians over the last two decades that
people almost expect their leaders to fall into some form of
immorality. It is shameful that our culture has practically lost
the ability to blush.

Just a cursory reading of the Old Testament will lead you to
realize that sex scandals have been around for a long time. And
the truth of the matter is, you don't have to be famous to fall
into sexual sin.

I believe one of the first steps toward sexual immorality is
isolationism. In our passage today, King David should have
been on the battleground with his men. He had no business
staying back at the palace and strolling around the rooftops

leering at bathing beauties. It appears that David was isolated from people and, we assume, unable to confide in trusted friends before he slept with Bathsheba. Trying to "do life" on your own and living free from any form of accountability can spell disaster for leaders and for ordinary people like you and me.

If you and your partner have made a pledge to remain celibate until marriage, then you must realize that you cannot accomplish this goal alone. It will take the power of the Spirit, clearly identified boundaries, and the loving support of friends to enable you to stand strong in your commitment. You must enlist the support of close, trusted friends who value purity and will encourage a life of integrity. Having these same-sex friends and meeting with them on a regular basis can make a radical difference in your life. Having a friend or an accountability group gives you the opportunity to pray for one another, confess your temptations, and encourage one another in your relationship with your partner.

We cannot emphasize enough the tremendous need we all have to be in community with others. Isolationism causes you to lose objectivity and perspective, and it separates you from the support of others. If you have a support group, or even one or two people in your life to open up with, you will discover that everyone tends to struggle with the same issues. We are convinced after nearly twenty years in the ministry and thousands of hours in one-on-one counseling situations that no one is smart enough, spiritual enough, or strong enough to do life on his own.

Do you have anyone in your life, other than your partner, with whom you can get real? Is there anyone or a group of same-gender friends holding you accountable to your commitment to practice sexual purity? If not, make it your top priority to recruit some help today. Pray that God would lead you to the right person, group, or counselor. Home alone can be a dangerous place to be. God has wonderful things in store for you through the channel of life-giving friendships.

FURTHER SCRIPTURAL MEDITATION
- Ecclesiastes 4:9–11
- 2 Timothy 2:22
- James 1:12–16

Summarize, in your own words, the essence of this day's devotional on purity. Write down any thoughts, feelings, or insights in the space below.

Dear God, help me to seek out safe, supportive, and trusted friends who will support my efforts to stay pure. Amen.

Purity and Forgiveness

Cleanse me with hyssop, and I will be clean;
wash me, and I will be whiter than snow.

—PSALM 51:7

*T*oo many have fallen outside the boundaries of healthy, righteous sexual expression at one time or another. For some the transition from adolescence to adulthood or the process of discovery tends to lead them to sample the sexual waters outside God's guidelines. For others there is the temptation to meet legitimate needs for intimacy in illegitimate ways. At the very least most can relate to what Jesus considers "adultery of the heart"—the ongoing struggle with lust or fantasy. In spite of how you feel about the issue of sex and regardless of the underlying cause, any form of sex outside the context of marriage is wrong, and God calls it sin.

Therefore, we must have a way to cleanse our minds and hearts. The only way to maintain the spirit of purity is to accept God's forgiveness and cleansing. When someone confesses a sexual sin, God cleanses him completely and makes him pure. Isaiah 1:18 affirms, "Though your sins are like scarlet, they shall be as white as snow."

Take a close look at Psalm 51. It represents King David's confession and repentance of his sin of adultery with Bathsheba. What you don't see in this passage from David is a casual reaction ("Gee whiz, I'm so sorry that I got caught"). What you do notice about this famous confession is the manner in which David took full responsibility for his sin. You find no excuses, rationalizations, or blame-shifting for his behavior. You observe his deep appreciation for the severity of his offenses. He understood that his sexual sin was serious and that it was a sin against God Himself. David fully recognized that only God could cleanse him and restore a pure heart. And you see in David a man who exhibited a genuine sense of remorse. He came before God with a broken spirit and a contrite heart. He had an emotional response to his sin against almighty God.

This is the example for receiving true forgiveness from God. By the way, no sexual sin is beyond the reach of God's infinite supply of grace and forgiveness. When it comes to forgiveness, don't get too hung up on where you've been, what you've done, or how many times you may have fallen. All He wants from you is a humble, repentant heart, and Christ's blood will take care of the rest.

It's never too late to receive God's forgiveness and reclaim your purity for the sake of your spiritual health and for your future marriage. Do you need to do business with God concerning confession of sexual sin? Take action today and reclaim what has been lost.

FURTHER SCRIPTURAL MEDITATION
- Psalm 51:1–10
- Psalm 119:9–11
- Isaiah 1:18

Summarize, in your own words, the essence of this day's devotional on purity. Write down any thoughts, feelings, or insights in the space below.

Father, I confess my sin, I accept Your forgiveness; cleanse me and make me pure. Thank You that true repentance always leads to purity. Amen.

Prayer

Dear Lord,

I praise You that You are a gracious and awesome Creator. In Your image and by Your design, we are fearfully and wonderfully made. Thank You for the gift of sexuality.

I confess that I have let the world devalue and corrupt my beliefs and attitudes about sex rather than let the truth of Your Word stand on its own. I realize that Your highest plan for sex is glorious, pure, and spiritual, and we often perceive it on merely a physical level. Lord, because of my devalued perception of sex and following my own desires, I confess that I have taken sex out of its proper context of holy marriage and have pushed the boundaries of respect and purity and have sinned against You. Thank You for Your faithfulness to forgive me even when I feel that I have gone beyond the limits of grace.

I pray that You would heal me of the damage this has caused in my heart and my emotions. Help me to establish clear boundaries in my current relationship, empower me with the Holy Spirit to follow through, and help me to find godly friends to hold me accountable.

In Jesus' name I pray. Amen.

Prayer Journal

PRAISE (ADORATION):

REPENTANCE (CONFESSION):

APPRECIATION (THANKSGIVING):

YIELD (REQUESTS):

A Foundation of Purity

*T*oday we would like to encourage you and your partner to set aside some time just for the two of you. We suggest you find a relaxing and peaceful setting to discuss the topic of *purity*. Keep in mind that the purpose is to ask questions, listen with compassion, and share with each other about your experiences regarding the issue for this past week. Remember, this is not a time to debate or argue about theological perspectives. This is a time to listen and seek to understand each other with a spirit of support and encouragement. Ultimately this venture together is intended to build a stronger foundation of spiritual intimacy.

This past week we have addressed the most delicate subject of purity. You have learned first and foremost that sex starts with God and is a precious gift that must be celebrated! You have identified the fact that God is crystal clear about the importance of saving sex for marriage. You've also discovered that His ideal for you (sex within the context of marriage) is for your own good—to maximize this wonderful and sacred gift. And you have been encouraged to embrace God's forgiveness and grace in order to cleanse you from past sexual sin and reclaim the spirit of purity.

QUESTIONS FOR DISCUSSION

1. How do you define *purity*?

2. Discuss how you feel about the issue of purity.

3. What are your convictions regarding the need to maintain purity within your relationship?

4. Are you satisfied with your physical boundaries and your method for controlling your passions within this relationship?

5. Have you ever discussed your need for guidelines or boundaries within this arena?

6. Are you in need of God's forgiveness and grace concerning this area of your life?

7. Do you, as a couple, need to confess your past indiscretions and seek God's cleansing?

8. If necessary, would you be willing to change your level of physical contact for the health and stability of your relationship?

SUNDAY

SERMON NOTES:

INSIGHTS TO SHARE:

The Spirit

Glory be to the Father, and to the Son, and to the Holy Spirit.

When the Spirit illuminates the heart,
then a part of the man sees which never saw before.

—A. W. TOZER

There is only One Being who can satisfy
the last aching abyss of the human heart,
and that is the Lord Jesus Christ.

—BLAISE PASCAL

Discipline imposed from the outside eventually
defeats when it is not matched by desire from within.

—DAWSON TROTMAN

The Power Source

You will receive power when the Holy Spirit comes on you; and you will be my witnesses in Jerusalem, and in all Judea and Samaria, and to the ends of the earth.

—ACTS 1:8

There is something noble about mowing your own grass. When I was a boy, our father bought my brother and me a yellow Kmart lawn mower. Just about every Saturday we pushed that cheap piece of tin back and forth to cut what seemed to be a football field of grass. When our family moved to Houston in 1978, we stopped mowing our own lawn. We were too busy chasing girls, playing basketball, and trying to graduate from high school to worry about the yard.

However, thirteen years later, I rented an old duplex with a backyard that felt as if it were the size of the state of California. When the grass grew to be fifteen feet high, I decided it was time to come out of my yard-maintenance retirement plan. I borrowed a mower from my uncle who lived a block away, and I pushed that heavy green Lawn-Boy back and forth until the task was complete.

Two weeks passed, and I found myself once again sweating, pushing, and pulling the Green Monster all over my yard until it happened. While I was attempting a U-turn, my hand slipped on the handlebars and seemingly bent the thing in two. Suddenly the lawn mower took off by itself as if it had a mind of its own. I felt like an idiot. Since I had not mowed a lawn in more than a decade, I was clueless about the self-propelled gems. I had exerted all of my strength and effort, gritting my teeth, sweat pouring down from my face like a waterfall, when all I had to do was guide the mower and let it do all the work.

Ironically we can glean a spiritual truth from my mowing experience. Too many times we try to live our Christian lives by our own effort and willpower. We sweat and toil daily to love our coworkers, stop a nagging habit, or resist a temptation that constantly knocks at our door. We live as if we must do all the work and forget about the power that God has placed inside us.

Before Jesus was crucified and rose from the dead, He told His followers that He was going to leave them. And after He ascended to the Father in heaven, Jesus sent the Holy Spirit to dwell in the hearts of men and women who would follow Him. The Holy Spirit would give them power, supernatural power to love, serve, and reach a lost and dying world.

If you have trusted in Jesus Christ, God's Holy Spirit lives inside you to empower you to live a life that will please Him. It is impossible to live a godly life in your own strength. It is impossible to obey the commandments of God by the sweat of your brow. It is impossible to love your neighbor, much less your enemies, without the power of the Spirit flowing through you. The great news is that the Holy Spirit does live in your heart and can empower you to love others, fight sin, and serve God with gladness. Romans 8:11 declares that the same power that raised Jesus from the dead lives in you. That's incredible!

Stop pushing and pulling and instead allow the power of the Spirit to live through you today. Say to the Lord, "I cannot live this Christian life on my own. I need You to live it through me today. Thank You that You have placed Your Spirit in my heart. Empower me right now to passionately live a life that would bring honor to You."

FURTHER SCRIPTURAL MEDITATION
- Zechariah 4:6
- Ephesians 6:10
- 1 John 4:4

Summarize, in your own words, the essence of this day's devotional on the Holy Spirit. Write down any thoughts, feelings, or insights in the space below.

Dear Father, I confess that in vain I try to live the Christian life by my own power. Teach me how to release control to the power of the Holy Spirit that lives in me so that my life would bring honor and glory to You. Amen.

Never Alone

I will ask the Father, and he will give you another Counselor to be with you forever—the Spirit of truth. The world cannot accept him, because it neither sees him nor knows him. But you know him, for he lives with you and will be in you. I will not leave you as orphans.

—JOHN 14:16–18

A friend of mine used to be a counselor at a sports camp in the mountains. The eleven-year-old boys in his cabin loved going down to the lake to face the challenge of jumping off the thirty-foot high dive into the ice-cold water below. The camp rule was: you climb to the top; you make the jump! Every summer at least one camper would get up the courage to climb the rungs to the top of the platform only to chicken out when he realized just how far he had to fall to hit the water.

To ensure quality control, the camp had a supporting rule, which stated that if a kid wouldn't take the leap by himself, his counselor would have to jump with him. Michael McGuire stood on the edge of the diving platform, terrified of the distance that separated him from the water below. His counselor scaled the ladder with great speed and told Michael to relax because he would make the jump with him. When the counselor finally reached him, Michael shook with fear. The counselor reached out and grabbed Michael's hand and said, "On the count of three, we are going to make this jump." So on three they jumped from the platform and splashed into the coffee black water. The bonding experience between Michael and his counselor was priceless.

Before the Romans crucified Jesus Christ, His disciples were trembling with fear, just like little Michael. When Jesus told His disciples that He was leaving to return to the Father, they were deeply afraid. Certainly they thought, *What will we do without You? How will we know the way? How can we face the opposition by ourselves?* Christ comforted them by saying, "Don't worry. I will not leave you as orphans. I will send the Holy Spirit to mediate My presence to you. He will not only be with you, as I am with you, but He will also be in you." In another passage of Scripture, He went on to say that it was better for Him to go so that He could send the Spirit.

Even if you have a personal relationship with Christ, you may feel lonely at times but be assured that you are never alone. The Holy Spirit is the Comforter who is with you right now to give you the strength, courage, and comfort you need today. Whether you feel like it or not, God is with you. Maybe you feel afraid to attack a challenge in your life, just as the camper did on the high dive. Let the Holy Spirit be your Counselor, take you by the hand, and give you the strength that you need to face this challenge.

Read this encouraging statement found in Matthew 28:20: "I am with you always, even to the end of the world" (PHILLIPS).

What an incredible promise! Do you believe that? Imagine what this day could hold in store for you if you would simply take God at His word and stand on the promise that He is with you and in you, by the power of His Spirit. When you embrace the fact that God is truly with you, He gives you the courage to face your greatest fears and to jump off any high dive with which life challenges you.

FURTHER SCRIPTURAL MEDITATION
- Isaiah 41:10
- John 16:7
- 1 John 4:13

Summarize, in your own words, the essence of this day's devotional on the Holy Spirit. Write down any thoughts, feelings, or insights in the space below.

God, I thank You that You have given us the Spirit to comfort and guide us. Help me to change the way that I live each day as I am mindful of Your daily presence in my life. Amen.

Who's in the Spotlight?

When he, the Spirit of truth, comes, he will guide you into all truth. He will not speak on his own; he will speak only what he hears, and he will tell you what is yet to come. He will bring glory to me by taking from what is mine and making it known to you.

—JOHN 16:13–14

For many years the church where I serve has put on a holiday spectacular called "The Singing Christmas Tree." A singing Christmas tree is a thirty-foot-tall steel structure shaped like a beautiful evergreen. The tree is filled with sixty choir members wearing Star Trek–like silver robes with bright red collars, and they joyfully sing the beloved Christmas songs of the faith.

One Christmas, a silver-haired woman named Tina was supposed to sing a special number, but the guy operating the spotlight that night inadvertently shone the light on Barbara (another gray-haired woman) about two rows under Tina. For a while, the only thing that the audience could see was Barbara basking in the glory of the spotlight while an unknown voice flowed out of the speakers.

After a minute or so, Barbara realized what was going on

and proceeded to lip-synch the song. The spotlight operator made a legitimate mistake that evening. He shone the light on the wrong person. A spotlight is meant to single out the star in a play or musical number, not someone who is playing a supporting role.

In his book *Keep in Step with the Spirit,* J. I. Packer compares the ministry of the Holy Spirit to a spotlight: "The Spirit's message to us is never, 'Look at me; listen to me; come to me; get to know me,' but always, 'Look at *him,* and see *his* glory; listen to *him,* and hear *his* word; go to *him,* and have life; get to know *him,* and taste *his* gift of joy and peace' . . . His ministry is a flood-light ministry in relation to Jesus, a matter of spotlighting Jesus' glory before our spiritual eyes and of matchmaking between us and him." The Holy Spirit seeks not to glorify Himself, but to glorify Jesus Christ.

As you look back on the day you trusted Jesus Christ as your Lord and Savior, you now realize that the Holy Spirit pulled back the curtain hanging over your eyes so that you could see Christ as your only hope for forgiveness and reconciliation with God. The Holy Spirit spotlights the work of Jesus Christ. He opens our blind eyes to see how wretched we are compared to the perfection of Christ. He shows us that only through faith in Christ can we be rescued from destruction and despair. And after our conversion, He mediates the presence of Christ to us day in and day out. You and I could never appreciate the power of spiritual intimacy with a partner or with God Himself without the work of the Holy Spirit.

Many times the Spirit is working in your life, and you don't even know it. But make no mistake about it; if the Holy Spirit is working in your life, He will always be pointing you to Jesus, not yourself or your accomplishments. Don't forget that the symbol of the Christian faith is the cross, and the third person in the Trinity will always be found spotlighting the saving work of Christ on that cross. Ask the Holy Spirit to make this truth real to you today and fill you with the presence of Jesus.

FURTHER SCRIPTURAL MEDITATION
- Ezekiel 36:26–27
- John 15:26
- 1 John 5:6–8

Summarize, in your own words, the essence of this day's devotional on the Holy Spirit. Write down any thoughts, feelings, or insights in the space below.

Dear Lord, I am grateful for the work of the Holy Spirit in my life although I so often neglect the truth of Your presence. Help me to always see the work of the Spirit pointing to the ways and the work of Jesus Christ. Amen.

The Spirit of Grace

He said to me, "My grace is sufficient for you, for my power is made perfect in weakness." Therefore I will boast all the more gladly about my weaknesses, so that Christ's power may rest on me.

—2 CORINTHIANS 12:9

Growing up in a preacher's home, I had the privilege of meeting many fascinating people. When I was in elementary school, one of the survivors of a Nazi concentration camp, Corrie ten Boom, came to our house for lunch following a Sunday morning worship service. Someone once asked Corrie how she was able to survive the horrors and torments of Hitler's death camp, and here is how she responded: "When I was a little girl growing up in Holland, the train was a primary means of transportation. If I had to take a trip to Amsterdam, my father would buy my ticket weeks in advance. However, he would not give me the ticket until the day of my journey, for fear that I might lose it." She explained how God did the same thing for her while she was in prison; He gave her just enough strength for that particular day and that particular challenge. Likewise, when the Israelites were stuck in the desert thousands of years ago, God rained down manna from heaven for their daily bread.

They could not save the manna, or it would spoil, so they had to remain dependent on God's daily supply.

It's wonderful to know that the same God who provided food for the Israelites in the desert and courage for Corrie ten Boom in prison provides for you and me as well. In our verse for today, Paul recounts God's response after he pleaded with Him to remove a mysterious "thorn in the flesh" causing him much pain and difficulty. Paul prayed to God three times to remove his thorn. How many times have you asked God to remove you from a tough situation or take away some excruciating pain? Jesus answered Paul's prayer by saying, "Look, I'm not going to remove this thorn, but I will empower you by My Spirit so others will see My divine power shining through your weakness." God promised to give Paul the all-sufficient, enabling grace of the Holy Spirit.

Perhaps you have a weakness in your life that you want God to remove. Maybe it's a tough family life, an emotional wound from the past, ridicule from others who don't understand your faith, or just the stress of making it through a hectic week at work or school. God will not always pull you out of a stressful scenario or zap the pain from your body, but He does promise to give you the grace of His Spirit, who is sufficient for the need of the moment.

As you look to the future and try to forecast all the trials and sufferings you may experience in this life, it's easy to become overwhelmed. Where will you find the strength to endure? How will you face the pain? How will you know what to do? God promises daily grace to you. When you are weak,

He is strong. Ask God to help you embrace this promise for today. Ask Him to meet all your needs in Christ Jesus. Pray that His power will shine through your weakness. Don't worry about tomorrow's journey. He will give you the ticket of grace when you need it.

FURTHER SCRIPTURAL MEDITATION
- Psalm 84:11
- Philippians 4:19
- Hebrews 4:15–16

Summarize, in your own words, the essence of this day's devotional on the Holy Spirit. Write down any thoughts, feelings, or insights in the space below.

Dear God, as each day brings new challenges, help me to remember Your daily grace. I pray that in each trial the grace of Your Spirit will shine through my weakness to bring You glory. Amen.

Living Under the Influence

Do not get drunk on wine, which leads to debauchery. Instead, be filled with the Spirit.

—EPHESIANS 5:18

The drinking of alcoholic beverages has been a divisive issue among Christians for centuries. Some feel that it's a sin to drink because it causes others to stumble and could lead to a possible addiction. Whose life has not been affected by a friend or family member who abused alcohol? Others reason that it's okay to drink as long as it is done in a responsible manner.

No matter where you stand on the issue, the Bible is clear about getting drunk—it is wrong. Period. In this verse, Paul compared being under the influence of alcohol to being under the influence of the Spirit.

Someone who is drunk is out of control and often unaware of what he is saying or doing. He is under the influence of another substance. When you are filled with the Holy Spirit, you are under His influence, but the end result is different. If you are filled with the Spirit, you will practice self-control, love, and compassion toward others.

In this passage, God gave us two commands: "Don't get

drunk" and "Be filled with the Spirit." Actually the final mandate means "to be continually filled with the Spirit," which implies that this is not a onetime experience. So, what does it mean to be filled with the Spirit? What does that look like and feel like?

There is no three-step formula for being filled with the Spirit. It's not as though you can see the low fuel light blinking on your spiritual dashboard and pull into your local filling station and fill your tank with divine premium fuel. Therefore, we'll attempt to describe this experience rather than prescribe a formula. When you are full of the Holy Spirit, you feel the things that God feels, and you desire the things that God desires. When you are full of the Holy Spirit, you love the way God loves, and you serve others the way God serves others. When you live daily by the Spirit, you sing to the Lord in your heart and give thanks to God the Father for everything. When you are filled with the Spirit, you humbly serve others for the sake of Christ.

How can you experience a fresh filling of God's Spirit? Ask Him. The Bible says that we have not because we ask not. But be careful. Are you sure you want to be filled? Do you really desire to be under the influence of another? Do you really want to relinquish that control? If you know Christ, you will yearn to be filled with His Spirit.

Pray that He will fill you daily with His Holy Spirit. Say, "I need You today. I need Your strength, Your power, and Your comfort. I cannot make it without You. Fill me with Your Spirit. Lead me today in all the decisions I have to make. Help me run from the things in my life that bring dishonor to Your name and bring me down as well. Thank You for this fresh touch. In Jesus' name. Amen." Now, go out and live under the influence of God's precious Holy Spirit.

FURTHER SCRIPTURAL MEDITATION
- Acts 1:8
- 1 Corinthians 3:16
- Galatians 5:16–25

Summarize, in your own words, the essence of this day's devotional on the Holy Spirit. Write down any thoughts, feelings, or insights in the space below.

Heavenly Father, today and every day I need Your strength, Your power, and Your comfort. I cannot make it without You. Fill me with Your Spirit. Lead me today in all the decisions I have to make and help me run from the things in my life that bring dishonor to Your name. Amen.

Prayer

Dear God,

I come into Your presence today through the grace You have given me through Jesus Christ. Without Christ, I could not know You, and I could never have the full assurance of forgiveness. Thank You that Your throne is one of grace and not one of works.

Lord, You promised never to leave us or forsake us, and through the indwelling power of Your Spirit, I know You are with me. How many times have I tried to live the Christian life in my own strength, only to fall flat on my face? I humbly thank You for picking me up off the pavement and showing me once again who is the Power Source of my life. You sent the Holy Spirit to live in me and to guide me into all truth. You sent the Spirit to spotlight the works of Jesus and to convince me of His righteousness.

Holy Spirit, I need You every second of every day. Produce Your fruit of love, joy, peace, patience, kindness, goodness, faithfulness, gentleness, and self-control through me. Fill me with Your strength and divine energy to follow God's will for my life. Thank You for convicting me when I sin, and for constantly communicating the presence of Christ to me.

In Jesus' name I pray. Amen.

Prayer Journal

PRAISE (ADORATION):

REPENTANCE (CONFESSION):

APPRECIATION (THANKSGIVING):

YIELD (REQUESTS):

A Foundation of the Spirit

*T*oday we invite you and your partner to find a relaxing and peaceful setting to discuss *the power of the Spirit.* Keep in mind that the purpose is to ask questions, listen with compassion, and share with each other about your experiences regarding the issue for this past week. It is not a time to debate or argue about theological perspectives. Seek to understand each other with a spirit of support and encouragement. Ultimately this venture together is intended to build a stronger foundation of spiritual intimacy.

The subject of the Holy Spirit is one of the most misunderstood topics of the Christian faith. Because He is so often neglected, some have dubbed the Holy Spirit the stepchild of the Trinity. Of course, the role of the Spirit is critical in the life of the believer. This past week, we have considered the notion that the Holy Spirit is a personal expression of God Himself and the very presence of God. When Christ ascended to heaven after His resurrection, the Holy Spirit descended as a replacement. You've been encouraged to consider some of the functions of the Holy Spirit including Counselor, Comforter, Mediator, Power Source, and others. Most important, you've come to understand that His primary role is to point others to Christ, just as a spotlight shines on the lead character in a play.

QUESTIONS FOR DISCUSSION

1. What is your history concerning the Holy Spirit? Did you grow up with an adequate understanding of His role and function?

2. Could you share with your partner a time when you felt a strong sense of the Holy Spirit's presence? Maybe you felt a real peace, comfort, or courage in the face of difficult circumstances. Discuss this particular time when you felt Him working in your life.

3. What is your interpretation of "being continually filled" with the Spirit? How would you explain this process for you?

4. What is your reaction to the "spotlight" analogy?

5. How can your partner help you become more aware of the presence and function of the Holy Spirit?

6. What else can you share with each other concerning this topic?

SUNDAY

SERMON NOTES:

INSIGHTS TO SHARE:

About the Authors

Ben Young, M.Div., author and speaker, leads seminars on how to build successful dating relationships. He hosts *The Single Connection,* a nationally syndicated radio show, and is an associate pastor at the 30,000-member Second Baptist Church in Houston, Texas. Ben and Sam Adams coauthored *The One* and bestselling *The Ten Commandments of Dating.*

Samuel Adams, Psy.D., is a licensed clinical psychologist. He earned a bachelor's degree from Baylor University, his master's from Western Seminary, and a doctorate from George Fox Graduate School of Clinical Psychology. He maintains a full-time counseling practice and is a relationship conference speaker. He lives in Austin, Texas, with his wife, Julie, and their three children.

The Single Connection
with Ben Young

If you want straight talk about relationships every week, tune into The Single Connection with your host Ben Young as he doles out free relationship advice each week and interviews the experts on love and relationships like Dr. Laura Schlessinger, Henry Cloud and John Townsend, Les Parrott, Neil Clark Warren, John Eldredge, Tommy Nelson, and many others. Ben Young is in touch and outspoken on all the hot topics that affect singles. He addresses it all, from dating to divorce and sex and cyber-porn. Don't miss The Single Connection, America's only live talk show just for singles. Tune in every Sunday night from 9–11 CST around the country and live on the Internet. Go to our web-site to find out more about the show and how to listen in your area.

www.benyoung.org

$\mathcal{D}$o you know anyone who is confused and frustrated about finding "the one"? If so, then have them check out Ben and Sam's bestselling *The Ten Commandments of Dating*. This book offers hard-hitting, black-and-white, practical guidelines that will address various questions about dating. This is not more relationship advice—it's relationship common sense.

The Ten Commandments of Dating

0-7852-7022-1

The Ten Commandments of Dating EZ Lesson Plan takes the practical advice of the book and goes a little deeper. It can be used for small groups, retreats, Sunday school, or individual study. The plan includes one video and audio tape and a facilitator's guide. Also available is *The Ten Commandments of Dating* Participant's Guide.

EZ Lesson Plan

0-7852-9619-0

Participant's Guide

0-7852-9621-2

$\mathcal{D}$o you have friends who think there is just one person God has for them? In *The One*, Ben and Sam offer a plainspoken and entertaining approach for individuals seeking to find the love of their life. *The One* gives three nonnegotiables in finding a soul mate and provides a five-question, instant compatibility test. Your friends will discover practical and spiritual wisdom in their quest for "The One."

The One

0-7852-6744-1

To order any of the above resources, you can contact your local Christian bookstore or log onto:

www.benyoung.org

or call

1-800-553-9772.